An Introduction to GCC

for the GNU Compilers gcc and g++
Revised and updated

Brian Gough
Foreword by Richard M. Stallman

A catalogue record for this book is available from the British Library.

Second printing, August 2005 (1/8/2005). Revised and updated.
First printing, March 2004 (7/3/2004).

Published by Network Theory Limited.

15 Royal Park
Bristol
BS8 3AL
United Kingdom

Email: info@network-theory.co.uk

ISBN 0-9541617-9-3

Further information about this book is available from
http://www.network-theory.co.uk/gcc/intro/

Cover Image: From a layout of a fast, energy-efficient hardware stack.[1]
Image created with the free Electric VLSI design system by Steven Rubin
of Static Free Software (www.staticfreesoft.com). Static Free Software
provides support for Electric to the electronics design industry.

The Texinfo source for this manual may be obtained from:
http://www.network-theory.co.uk/gcc/intro/src/

---

[1] "A Fast and Energy-Efficient Stack" by J. Ebergen, D. Finchelstein, R. Kao,
J. Lexau and R. Hopkins.

Table of Contents

Foreword

This foreword has been kindly contributed by Richard M. Stallman, the principal author of GCC and founder of the GNU Project.

This book is a guide to getting started with GCC, the GNU Compiler Collection. It will tell you how to use GCC as a programming tool. GCC is a programming tool, that's true—but it is also something more. It is part of a 20-year campaign for freedom for computer users.

We all want good software, but what does it mean for software to be "good"? Convenient features and reliability are what it means to be *technically* good, but that is not enough. Good software must also be *ethically* good: it has to respect the users' freedom.

As a user of software, you should have the right to run it as you see fit, the right to study the source code and then change it as you see fit, the right to redistribute copies of it to others, and the right to publish a modified version so that you can contribute to building the community. When a program respects your freedom in this way, we call it *free software*. Before GCC, there were other compilers for C, Fortran, Ada, etc. But they were not free software; you could not use them in freedom. I wrote GCC so we could use a compiler without giving up our freedom.

A compiler alone is not enough—to use a computer system, you need a whole operating system. In 1983, all operating systems for modern computers were non-free. To remedy this, in 1984 I began developing the GNU operating system, a Unix-like system that would be free software. Developing GCC was one part of developing GNU.

By the early 90s, the nearly-finished GNU operating system was completed by the addition of a kernel, Linux, that became free software in 1992. The combined GNU/Linux operating system has achieved the goal of making it possible to use a computer in freedom. But freedom is never automatically secure, and we need to work to defend it. The Free Software Movement needs your support.

Richard M. Stallman
February 2004

1 Introduction

The purpose of this book is to explain the use of the GNU C and C++ compilers, gcc and g++. After reading this book you should understand how to compile a program, and how to use basic compiler options for optimization and debugging. This book does not attempt to teach the C or C++ languages themselves, since this material can be found in many other places (see [Further reading], page 111).

Experienced programmers who are familiar with other systems, but new to the GNU compilers, can skip the early sections of the chapters "*Compiling a C program*", "*Using the preprocessor*" and "*Compiling a C++ program*". The remaining sections and chapters should provide a good overview of the features of GCC for those already know how to use other compilers.

1.1 A brief history of GCC

The original author of the GNU C Compiler (GCC) is Richard Stallman, the founder of the GNU Project.

The GNU Project was started in 1984 to create a complete Unix-like operating system as free software, in order to promote freedom and cooperation among computer users and programmers. Every Unix-like operating system needs a C compiler, and as there were no free compilers in existence at that time, the GNU Project had to develop one from scratch. The work was funded by donations from individuals and companies to the Free Software Foundation, a non-profit organization set up to support the work of the GNU Project.

The first release of GCC was made in 1987. This was a significant breakthrough, being the first portable ANSI C optimizing compiler released as free software. Since that time GCC has become one of the most important tools in the development of free software.

A major revision of the compiler came with the 2.0 series in 1992, which added the ability to compile C++. In 1997 an experimental branch of the compiler (EGCS) was created, to improve optimization and C++ support. Following this work, EGCS was adopted as the new main-line of GCC development, and these features became widely available in the 3.0 release of GCC in 2001.

Over time GCC has been extended to support many additional languages, including Fortran, ADA, Java and Objective-C. The acronym GCC is now used to refer to the "GNU Compiler Collection". Its development is guided by the *GCC Steering Committee*, a group composed

of representatives from GCC user communities in industry, research and
academia.

1.2 Major features of GCC

This section describes some of the most important features of GCC.

First of all, GCC is a portable compiler—it runs on most platforms
available today, and can produce output for many types of processors. In
addition to the processors used in personal computers, it also supports
microcontrollers, DSPs and 64-bit CPUs.

GCC is not only a native compiler—it can also *cross-compile* any program, producing executable files for a different system from the one used
by GCC itself. This allows software to be compiled for embedded systems
which are not capable of running a compiler. GCC is written in C with
a strong focus on portability, and can compile itself, so it can be adapted
to new systems easily.

GCC has multiple language *frontends*, for parsing different languages.
Programs in each language can be compiled, or cross-compiled, for any
architecture. For example, an ADA program can be compiled for a mi-
crocontroller, or a C program for a supercomputer.

GCC has a modular design, allowing support for new languages and
architectures to be added. Adding a new language front-end to GCC
enables the use of that language on any architecture, provided that the
necessary run-time facilities (such as libraries) are available. Similarly,
adding support for a new architecture makes it available to all languages.

Finally, and most importantly, GCC is free software, distributed under
the GNU General Public License (GNU GPL).[1] This means you have
the freedom to use and to modify GCC, as with all GNU software. If you
need support for a new type of CPU, a new language, or a new feature
you can add it yourself, or hire someone to enhance GCC for you. You
can hire someone to fix a bug if it is important for your work.

Furthermore, you have the freedom to share any enhancements you
make to GCC. As a result of this freedom you can also make use of
enhancements to GCC developed by others. The many features offered
by GCC today show how this freedom to cooperate works to benefit you,
and everyone else who uses GCC.

1.3 Programming in C and C++

C and C++ are languages that allow direct access to the computer's memory. Historically, they have been used for writing low-level systems soft-

---

[1] For details see the license file 'COPYING' distributed with GCC.

ware, and applications where high-performance or control over resource usage are critical. However, great care is required to ensure that memory is accessed correctly, to avoid corrupting other data-structures. This book describes techniques that will help in detecting potential errors during compilation, but the risk in using languages like C or C++ can never be eliminated.

In addition to C and C++ the GNU Project also provides other high-level languages, such as GNU Common Lisp (gcl), GNU Smalltalk (gst), the GNU Scheme extension language (guile) and the GNU Compiler for Java (gcj). These languages do not allow the user to access memory directly, eliminating the possibility of memory access errors. They are a safer alternative to C and C++ for many applications.

1.4 Conventions used in this manual

This manual contains many examples which can be typed at the keyboard. A command entered at the terminal is shown like this,

```
$ command
```

followed by its output. For example:

```
$ echo "hello world"
hello world
```

The first character on the line is the terminal prompt, and should not be typed. The dollar sign '$' is used as the standard prompt in this manual, although some systems may use a different character.

When a command in an example is too long to fit in a single line it is wrapped and then indented on subsequent lines, like this:

```
$ echo "an example of a line which is too long to fit
    in this manual"
```

When entered at the keyboard, the entire command should be typed on a single line.

The example source files used in this manual can be downloaded from the publisher's website,[2] or entered by hand using any text editor, such as the standard GNU editor, emacs. The example compilation commands use gcc and g++ as the names of the GNU C and C++ compilers, and cc to refer to other compilers. The example programs should work with any version of GCC. Any command-line options which are only available in recent versions of GCC are noted in the text.

The examples assume the use of a GNU operating system—there may be minor differences in the output on other systems. Some non-essential and verbose system-dependent output messages (such as very long system

---

[2] See http://www.network-theory.co.uk/gcc/intro/

paths) have been edited in the examples for brevity. The commands for setting environment variables use the syntax of the standard GNU shell (bash), and should work with any version of the Bourne shell.

2 Compiling a C program

This chapter describes how to compile C programs using gcc. Programs can be compiled from a single source file or from multiple source files, and may use system libraries and header files.

Compilation refers to the process of converting a program from the textual *source code*, in a programming language such as C or C++, into *machine code*, the sequence of 1's and 0's used to control the central processing unit (CPU) of the computer. This machine code is then stored in a file known as an *executable file*, sometimes referred to as a *binary file*.

2.1 Compiling a simple C program

The classic example program for the C language is *Hello World*. Here is the source code for our version of the program:

```
#include <stdio.h>

int
main (void)
{
  printf ("Hello, world!\n");
  return 0;
}
```

We will assume that the source code is stored in a file called 'hello.c'. To compile the file 'hello.c' with gcc, use the following command:

```
$ gcc -Wall hello.c -o hello
```

This compiles the source code in 'hello.c' to machine code and stores it in an executable file 'hello'. The output file for the machine code is specified using the '-o' option. This option is usually given as the last argument on the command line. If it is omitted, the output is written to a default file called 'a.out'.

Note that if a file with the same name as the executable file already exists in the current directory it will be overwritten.

The option '-Wall' turns on all the most commonly-used compiler warnings—**it is recommended that you always use this option!** There are many other warning options which will be discussed in later chapters, but '-Wall' is the most important. GCC will not produce any warnings unless they are enabled. Compiler warnings are an essential aid in detecting problems when programming in C and C++.

In this case, the compiler does not produce any warnings with the
'-Wall' option, since the program is completely valid. Source code which
does not produce any warnings is said to *compile cleanly*.

To run the program, type the path name of the executable like this:

```
$ ./hello
Hello, world!
```

This loads the executable file into memory and causes the CPU to begin
executing the instructions contained within it. The path ./ refers to the
current directory, so ./hello loads and runs the executable file 'hello'
located in the current directory.

2.2 Finding errors in a simple program

As mentioned above, compiler warnings are an essential aid when programming in C and C++. To demonstrate this, the program below contains a subtle error: it uses the function printf incorrectly, by specifying
a floating-point format '%f' for an integer value:

```
#include <stdio.h>

int
main (void)
{
  printf ("Two plus two is %f\n", 4);
  return 0;
}
```

This error is not obvious at first sight, but can be detected by the compiler
if the warning option '-Wall' has been enabled.

Compiling the program above, 'bad.c', with the warning option
'-Wall' produces the following message:

```
$ gcc -Wall bad.c -o bad
bad.c: In function 'main':
bad.c:6: warning: double format, different
   type arg (arg 2)
```

This indicates that a format string has been used incorrectly in the file
'bad.c' at line 6. The messages produced by GCC always have the form
file:line-number:message. The compiler distinguishes between *error messages*, which prevent successful compilation, and *warning messages* which
indicate possible problems (but do not stop the program from compiling).

In this case, the correct format specifier should be '%d' for an integer
argument. The allowed format specifiers for printf can be found in any
general book on C, such as the *GNU C Library Reference Manual* (see
[Further reading], page 111).

Without the warning option '-Wall' the program appears to compile cleanly, but produces incorrect results:

```
$ gcc bad.c -o bad
$ ./bad
Two plus two is 2.585495    (incorrect output)
```

The incorrect format specifier causes the output to be corrupted, because the function printf is passed an integer instead of a floating-point number. Integers and floating-point numbers are stored in different formats in memory, and generally occupy different numbers of bytes, leading to a spurious result. The actual output shown above may differ, depending on the specific platform and environment.

Clearly, it is very dangerous to develop a program without checking for compiler warnings. If there are any functions which are not used correctly they can cause the program to crash or produce incorrect results. Turning on the compiler warning option '-Wall' will catch many of the commonest errors which occur in C programming.

2.3 Compiling multiple source files

A program can be split up into multiple files. This makes it easier to edit and understand, especially in the case of large programs—it also allows the individual parts to be compiled independently.

In the following example we will split up the program *Hello World* into three files: 'main.c', 'hello_fn.c' and the header file 'hello.h'. Here is the main program 'main.c':

```
#include "hello.h"

int
main (void)
{
  hello ("world");
  return 0;
}
```

The original call to the printf system function in the previous program 'hello.c' has been replaced by a call to a new external function hello, which we will define in a separate file 'hello_fn.c'.

The main program also includes the header file 'hello.h' which will contain the declaration of the function hello. The declaration is used to ensure that the types of the arguments and return value match up correctly between the function call and the function definition. We no longer need to include the system header file 'stdio.h' in 'main.c' to declare the function `printf`, since the file 'main.c' does not call `printf` directly.

The declaration in 'hello.h' is a single line specifying the prototype of the function `hello`:

```
void hello (const char * name);
```

The definition of the function `hello` itself is contained in the file 'hello_fn.c':

```
#include <stdio.h>
#include "hello.h"

void
hello (const char * name)
{
  printf ("Hello, %s!\n", name);
}
```

This function prints the message "Hello, *name*!" using its argument as the value of *name*.

Incidentally, the difference between the two forms of the include statement `#include "FILE.h"` and `#include <FILE.h>` is that the former searches for 'FILE.h' in the current directory before looking in the system header file directories. The include statement `#include <FILE.h>` searches the system header files, but does not look in the current directory by default.

To compile these source files with gcc, use the following command:

```
$ gcc -Wall main.c hello_fn.c -o newhello
```

In this case, we use the '-o' option to specify a different output file for the executable, 'newhello'. Note that the header file 'hello.h' is not specified in the list of files on the command line. The directive `#include "hello.h"` in the source files instructs the compiler to include it automatically at the appropriate points.

To run the program, type the path name of the executable:

```
$ ./newhello
Hello, world!
```

All the parts of the program have been combined into a single executable file, which produces the same result as the executable created from the single source file used earlier.

2.4 Compiling files independently

If a program is stored in a single file then any change to an individual function requires the whole program to be recompiled to produce a new executable. The recompilation of large source files can be very time-consuming.

When programs are stored in independent source files, only the files which have changed need to be recompiled after the source code has been modified. In this approach, the source files are compiled separately and then *linked* together—a two stage process. In the first stage, a file is compiled without creating an executable. The result is referred to as an *object file*, and has the extension '.o' when using GCC.

In the second stage, the object files are merged together by a separate program called the *linker*. The linker combines all the object files to create a single executable.

An object file contains machine code where any references to the memory addresses of functions (or variables) in other files are left undefined. This allows source files to be compiled without direct reference to each other. The linker fills in these missing addresses when it produces the executable.

2.4.1 Creating object files from source files

The command-line option '-c' is used to compile a source file to an object file. For example, the following command will compile the source file 'main.c' to an object file:

```
$ gcc -Wall -c main.c
```

This produces an object file 'main.o' containing the machine code for the main function. It contains a reference to the external function hello, but the corresponding memory address is left undefined in the object file at this stage (it will be filled in later by linking).

The corresponding command for compiling the hello function in the source file 'hello_fn.c' is:

```
$ gcc -Wall -c hello_fn.c
```

This produces the object file 'hello_fn.o'.

Note that there is no need to use the option '-o' to specify the name of the output file in this case. When compiling with '-c' the compiler automatically creates an object file whose name is the same as the source file, but with '.o' instead of the original extension.

There is no need to put the header file 'hello.h' on the command line, since it is automatically included by the #include statements in 'main.c' and 'hello_fn.c'.

2.4.2 Creating executables from object files

The final step in creating an executable file is to use gcc to link the object files together and fill in the missing addresses of external functions. To link object files together, they are simply listed on the command line:

```
$ gcc main.o hello_fn.o -o hello
```

This is one of the few occasions where there is no need to use the '-Wall' warning option, since the individual source files have already been successfully compiled to object code. Once the source files have been compiled, linking is an unambiguous process which either succeeds or fails (it fails only if there are references which cannot be resolved).

To perform the linking step gcc uses the linker ld, which is a separate program. On GNU systems the GNU linker, GNU ld, is used. Other systems may use the GNU linker with GCC, or may have their own linkers. The linker itself will be discussed later (see Chapter 11 [How the compiler works], page 89). By running the linker, gcc creates an executable file from the object files.

The resulting executable file can now be run:

```
$ ./hello
Hello, world!
```

It produces the same output as the version of the program using a single source file in the previous section.

2.5 Recompiling and relinking

To show how source files can be compiled independently we will edit the main program 'main.c' and modify it to print a greeting to everyone instead of world:

```
#include "hello.h"

int
main (void)
{
  hello ("everyone");  /* changed from "world" */
  return 0;
}
```

The updated file 'main.c' can now be recompiled with the following command:

```
$ gcc -Wall -c main.c
```

This produces a new object file 'main.o'. There is no need to create a new object file for 'hello_fn.c', since that file and the related files that it depends on, such as header files, have not changed.

The new object file can be relinked with the `hello` function to create a new executable file:

```
$ gcc main.o hello_fn.o -o hello
```

The resulting executable 'hello' now uses the new `main` function to produce the following output:

```
$ ./hello
Hello, everyone!
```

Note that only the file 'main.c' has been recompiled, and then relinked with the existing object file for the `hello` function. If the file 'hello_fn.c' had been modified instead, we could have recompiled 'hello_fn.c' to create a new object file 'hello_fn.o' and relinked this with the existing file 'main.o'.[1]

In a large project with many source files, recompiling only those that have been modified can make a significant saving. The process of recompiling only the modified files in a project can be automated with the standard Unix program make.

2.6 A simple makefile

For those unfamiliar with make, this section provides a simple demonstration of its use. Make is a program in its own right and can be found on all Unix systems. To learn more about the GNU version of make you will need to consult the *GNU Make* manual by Richard M. Stallman and Roland McGrath (see [Further reading], page 111).

Make reads a description of a project from a *makefile* (by default, called 'Makefile' in the current directory). A makefile specifies a set of compilation rules in terms of *targets* (such as executables) and their *dependencies* (such as object files and source files) in the following format:

```
target: dependencies
        command
```

For each target, make checks the modification time of the corresponding dependency files to determine whether the target needs to be rebuilt using the corresponding command. Note that the *command* lines in a makefile must be indented with a single (TAB) character, not spaces.

GNU Make contains many default rules, referred to as *implicit* rules, to simplify the construction of makefiles. For example, these specify that '.o' files can be obtained from '.c' files by compilation, and that an executable can be made by linking together '.o' files. Implicit rules are defined in terms of *make variables*, such as CC (the C compiler) and CFLAGS

---

[1] If the prototype of a function has changed, it is necessary to modify and recompile all of the other source files which use it.

(the compilation options for C programs), which can be set using VARI-
ABLE=VALUE lines in the makefile. For C++ the equivalent variables are
CXX and CXXFLAGS, while the make variable CPPFLAGS sets the preprocessor options. The implicit and user-defined rules are automatically chained
together as necessary by GNU Make.

A simple 'Makefile' for the project above can be written as follows:

```
CC=gcc
CFLAGS=-Wall
main: main.o hello_fn.o

clean:
        rm -f main main.o hello_fn.o
```

The file can be read like this: using the C compiler gcc, with compilation
option '-Wall', build the target executable main from the object files
'main.o' and 'hello_fn.o' (these, in turn, will be built via implicit rules
from 'main.c' and 'hello_fn.c'). The target clean has no dependencies
and simply removes all the compiled files.[2] The option '-f' (force) on
the rm command suppresses any error messages if the files do not exist.

To use the makefile, type make. When called with no arguments, the
first target in the makefile is built, producing the executable 'main':

```
$ make
gcc -Wall    -c -o main.o main.c
gcc -Wall    -c -o hello_fn.o hello_fn.c
gcc    main.o hello_fn.o    -o main
$ ./main
Hello, world!
```

To rebuild the executable after modifying a source file, simply type make
again. By checking the timestamps of the target and dependency files,
make identifies the files which have changed and regenerates the corresponding intermediate files needed to update the targets:

```
$ emacs main.c   (edit the file)
$ make
gcc -Wall    -c -o main.o main.c
gcc    main.o hello_fn.o    -o main
$ ./main
Hello, everyone!
```

Finally, to remove the generated files, type make clean:

```
$ make clean
rm -f main main.o hello_fn.o
```

---

[2] This assumes that there is no file called 'clean' in the current directory—see
the discussion of "phony targets" in the GNU Make manual for details.

A more sophisticated makefile would usually contain additional targets for installation (make install) and testing (make check).

The examples in the rest of this book are small enough not to need makefiles, but the use of make is recommended for any larger programs.

2.7 Linking with external libraries

A library is a collection of precompiled object files which can be linked into programs. The most common use of libraries is to provide system functions, such as the square root function sqrt found in the C math library.

Libraries are typically stored in special *archive files* with the extension '.a', referred to as *static libraries*. They are created from object files with a separate tool, the GNU archiver ar, and used by the linker to resolve references to functions at compile-time. We will see later how to create libraries using the ar command (see Chapter 10 [Compiler-related tools], page 81). For simplicity, only static libraries are covered in this section— dynamic linking at runtime using *shared libraries* will be described in the next chapter.

The standard system libraries are usually found in the directories '/usr/lib' and '/lib'.[3] For example, the C math library is typically stored in the file '/usr/lib/libm.a' on Unix-like systems. The corresponding prototype declarations for the functions in this library are given in the header file '/usr/include/math.h'. The C standard library itself is stored in '/usr/lib/libc.a' and contains functions specified in the ANSI/ISO C standard, such as 'printf'—this library is linked by default for every C program.

Here is an example program which makes a call to the external function sqrt in the math library 'libm.a':

```
#include <math.h>
#include <stdio.h>

int
main (void)
{
  double x = sqrt (2.0);
  printf ("The square root of 2.0 is %f\n", x);
  return 0;
}
```

---

[3] On systems supporting both 64 and 32-bit executables the 64-bit versions of the libraries will often be stored in '/usr/lib64' and '/lib64', with the 32-bit versions in '/usr/lib' and '/lib'.

Trying to create an executable from this source file alone causes the compiler to give an error at the link stage:

```
$ gcc -Wall calc.c -o calc
/tmp/ccbR60jm.o: In function 'main':
/tmp/ccbR60jm.o(.text+0x19): undefined reference
   to 'sqrt'
```

The problem is that the reference to the sqrt function cannot be resolved without the external math library 'libm.a'. The function sqrt is not defined in the program or the default library 'libc.a', and the compiler does not link to the file 'libm.a' unless it is explicitly selected. Incidentally, the file mentioned in the error message '/tmp/ccbR60jm.o' is a temporary object file created by the compiler from 'calc.c', in order to carry out the linking process.

To enable the compiler to link the sqrt function to the main program 'calc.c' we need to supply the library 'libm.a'. One obvious but cumbersome way to do this is to specify it explicitly on the command line:

```
$ gcc -Wall calc.c /usr/lib/libm.a -o calc
```

The library 'libm.a' contains object files for all the mathematical functions, such as sin, cos, exp, log and sqrt. The linker searches through these to find the object file containing the sqrt function.

Once the object file for the sqrt function has been found, the main program can be linked and a complete executable produced:

```
$ ./calc
The square root of 2.0 is 1.414214
```

The executable file includes the machine code for the main function and the machine code for the sqrt function, copied from the corresponding object file in the library 'libm.a'.

To avoid the need to specify long paths on the command line, the compiler provides a short-cut option '-l' for linking against libraries. For example, the following command,

```
$ gcc -Wall calc.c -lm -o calc
```

is equivalent to the original command above using the full library name '/usr/lib/libm.a'.

In general, the compiler option '-l*NAME*' will attempt to link object files with a library file 'lib*NAME*.a' in the standard library directories. Additional directories can specified with command-line options and environment variables, to be discussed shortly. A large program will typically use many '-l' options to link libraries such as the math library, graphics libraries and networking libraries.

2.7.1 Link order of libraries

The traditional behavior of linkers is to search for external functions from left to right in the libraries specified on the command line. This means that a library containing the definition of a function should appear after any source files or object files which use it. This includes libraries specified with the short-cut '-l' option, as shown in the following command:

```
$ gcc -Wall calc.c -lm -o calc     (correct order)
```

With some linkers the opposite ordering (placing the '-lm' option before the file which uses it) would result in an error,

```
$ cc -Wall -lm calc.c -o calc      (incorrect order)
main.o: In function 'main':
main.o(.text+0xf): undefined reference to 'sqrt'
```

because there is no library or object file containing sqrt after 'calc.c'. The option '-lm' should appear after the file 'calc.c'.

When several libraries are being used, the same convention should be followed for the libraries themselves. A library which calls an external function defined in another library should appear before the library containing the function.

For example, a program 'data.c' using the GNU Linear Programming library 'libglpk.a', which in turn uses the math library 'libm.a', should be compiled as,

```
$ gcc -Wall data.c -lglpk -lm
```

since the object files in 'libglpk.a' use functions defined in 'libm.a'.

Most current linkers will search all libraries, regardless of order, but since some do not do this it is best to follow the convention of ordering libraries from left to right.

This is worth keeping in mind if you ever encounter unexpected problems with undefined references, and all the necessary libraries appear to be present on the command line.

2.8 Using library header files

When using a library it is essential to include the appropriate header files, in order to declare the function arguments and return values with the correct types. Without declarations, the arguments of a function can be passed with the wrong type, causing corrupted results.

The following example shows another program which makes a function call to the C math library. In this case, the function pow is used to compute the cube of two (2 raised to the power of 3):

```
#include <stdio.h>
```

```
int
main (void)
{
  double x = pow (2.0, 3.0);
  printf ("Two cubed is %f\n", x);
  return 0;
}
```

However, the program contains an error—the #include statement for 'math.h' is missing, so the prototype double pow (double x, double y) given there will not be seen by the compiler.

Compiling the program without any warning options will produce an executable file which gives incorrect results:

```
$ gcc badpow.c -lm
$ ./a.out
Two cubed is 2.851120     (incorrect result, should be 8)
```

The results are corrupted because the arguments and return value of the call to pow are passed with incorrect types.[4] This can be detected by turning on the warning option '-Wall':

```
$ gcc -Wall badpow.c -lm
badpow.c: In function 'main':
badpow.c:6: warning: implicit declaration of
  function 'pow'
```

This example shows again the importance of using the warning option '-Wall' to detect serious problems that could otherwise easily be overlooked.

---

[4] The actual output shown above may differ, depending on the specific platform and environment.

3 Compilation options

This chapter describes other commonly-used compiler options available in GCC. These options control features such as the search paths used for locating libraries and include files, the use of additional warnings and diagnostics, preprocessor macros and C language dialects.

3.1 Setting search paths

In the last chapter, we saw how to link to a program with functions in the C math library 'libm.a', using the short-cut option '-lm' and the header file 'math.h'.

A common problem when compiling a program using library header files is the error:

        FILE.h: No such file or directory

This occurs if a header file is not present in the standard include file directories used by gcc. A similar problem can occur for libraries:

        /usr/bin/ld: cannot find *library*

This happens if a library used for linking is not present in the standard library directories used by gcc.

By default, gcc searches the following directories for header files:

        /usr/local/include/
        /usr/include/

and the following directories for libraries:

        /usr/local/lib/
        /usr/lib/

The list of directories for header files is often referred to as the *include path*, and the list of directories for libraries as the *library search path* or *link path*.

The directories on these paths are searched in order, from first to last in the two lists above.[1]   For example, a header file found in '/usr/local/include' takes precedence over a file with the same name in '/usr/include'. Similarly, a library found in '/usr/local/lib' takes precedence over a library with the same name in '/usr/lib'.

When additional libraries are installed in other directories it is necessary to extend the search paths, in order for the libraries to be found.

---

[1] The default search paths may also include additional system-dependent or site-specific directories, and directories in the GCC installation itself. For example, on 64-bit platforms additional 'lib64' directories may also be searched by default.

The compiler options '-I' and '-L' add new directories to the beginning
of the include path and library search path respectively.

3.1.1 Search path example

The following example program uses a library that might be installed
as an additional package on a system—the GNU Database Management
Library (GDBM). The GDBM Library stores key-value pairs in a DBM
file, a type of data file which allows values to be stored and indexed by a
key (an arbitrary sequence of characters). Here is the example program
'dbmain.c', which creates a DBM file containing a key 'testkey' with the
value 'testvalue':

```
#include <stdio.h>
#include <gdbm.h>

int
main (void)
{
  GDBM_FILE dbf;
  datum key = { "testkey", 7 };      /* key, length */
  datum value = { "testvalue", 9 }; /* value, length */

  printf ("Storing key-value pair... ");
  dbf = gdbm_open ("test", 0, GDBM_NEWDB, 0644, 0);
  gdbm_store (dbf, key, value, GDBM_INSERT);
  gdbm_close (dbf);
  printf ("done.\n");
  return 0;
}
```

The program uses the header file 'gdbm.h' and the library 'libgdbm.a'. If
the library has been installed in the default location of '/usr/local/lib',
with the header file in '/usr/local/include', then the program can be
compiled with the following simple command:

```
$ gcc -Wall dbmain.c -lgdbm
```

Both these directories are part of the default gcc include and link paths.

However, if GDBM has been installed in a different location, trying to
compile the program will give the following error:

```
$ gcc -Wall dbmain.c -lgdbm
dbmain.c:1: gdbm.h: No such file or directory
```

For example, if version 1.8.3 of the GDBM package is installed under the
directory '/opt/gdbm-1.8.3' the location of the header file would be,

```
/opt/gdbm-1.8.3/include/gdbm.h
```

which is not part of the default gcc include path. Adding the appropriate
directory to the include path with the command-line option '-I' allows
the program to be compiled, but not linked:

```
$ gcc -Wall -I/opt/gdbm-1.8.3/include dbmain.c -lgdbm
/usr/bin/ld: cannot find -lgdbm
collect2: ld returned 1 exit status
```

The directory containing the library is still missing from the link path. It
can be added to the link path using the following option:

```
-L/opt/gdbm-1.8.3/lib/
```

The following command line allows the program to be compiled and linked:

```
$ gcc -Wall -I/opt/gdbm-1.8.3/include
    -L/opt/gdbm-1.8.3/lib dbmain.c -lgdbm
```

This produces the final executable linked to the GDBM library. Before
seeing how to run this executable we will take a brief look at the environment variables that affect the '-I' and '-L' options.

Note that you should never place the absolute paths of header files in
#include statements in your source code, as this will prevent the program
from compiling on other systems. The '-I' option or the INCLUDE_PATH
variable described below should always be used to set the include path for
header files.

3.1.2 Environment variables

The search paths for header files and libraries can also be controlled
through environment variables in the shell. These may be set automatically for each session using the appropriate login file, such as
'.bash_profile' in the case of GNU Bash.

Additional directories can be added to the include path using the environment variable C_INCLUDE_PATH (for C header files) or CPLUS_INCLUDE_
PATH (for C++ header files). For example, the following commands will
add '/opt/gdbm-1.8.3/include' to the include path when compiling C
programs:

```
$ C_INCLUDE_PATH=/opt/gdbm-1.8.3/include
$ export C_INCLUDE_PATH
```

and similarly for C++ programs:

```
$ CPLUS_INCLUDE_PATH=/opt/gdbm-1.8.3/include
$ export CPLUS_INCLUDE_PATH
```

This directory will be searched after any directories specified on the command line with the option '-I', and before the standard default directories
(such as '/usr/local/include' and '/usr/include'). The shell command export is needed to make the environment variable available to

programs outside the shell itself, such as the compiler—it is only needed once for each variable in each shell session, and can also be set in the appropriate login file.[2]

Similarly, additional directories can be added to the link path using the environment variable LIBRARY_PATH. For example, the following commands will add '/opt/gdbm-1.8.3/lib' to the link path:

```
$ LIBRARY_PATH=/opt/gdbm-1.8.3/lib
$ export LIBRARY_PATH
```

This directory will be searched after any directories specified on the command line with the option '-L', and before the standard default directories (such as '/usr/local/lib' and '/usr/lib').

With the environment variable settings given above the program 'dbmain.c' can be compiled without the '-I' and '-L' options,

```
$ gcc -Wall dbmain.c -lgdbm
```

because the default paths now use the directories specified in the environment variables C_INCLUDE_PATH and LIBRARY_PATH. The same compilation command with g++ would use the environment variables CPLUS_INCLUDE_PATH and LIBRARY_PATH.

3.1.3 Extended search paths

Following the standard Unix convention for search paths, several directories can be specified together in an environment variable as a colon separated list:

```
DIR1:DIR2:DIR3:...
```

The directories are then searched in order from left to right. A single dot '.' can be used to specify the current directory.[3]

For example, the following settings create default include and link paths for packages installed in the current directory '.' and the 'include' and 'lib' directories under '/opt/gdbm-1.8.3' and '/net' respectively:

```
$ C_INCLUDE_PATH=.:/opt/gdbm-1.8.3/include:/net/include
$ LIBRARY_PATH=.:/opt/gdbm-1.8.3/lib:/net/lib
```

For C++ programs, use the environment variable CPLUS_INCLUDE_PATH instead of C_INCLUDE_PATH.

To specify multiple search path directories on the command line, the options '-I' and '-L' can be repeated. For example, the following command,

---

[2] In GNU Bash, the shorter form export *VARIABLE=VALUE* is also allowed.

[3] The current directory can also be specified using an empty path element. For example, :*DIR1*:*DIR2* is equivalent to .:*DIR1*:*DIR2*.

```
$ gcc -I. -I/opt/gdbm-1.8.3/include -I/net/include
    -L. -L/opt/gdbm-1.8.3/lib -L/net/lib .....
```
is equivalent to the environment variable settings given above.

When environment variables and command-line options are used together the compiler searches the directories in the following order:

1. command-line options '-I' and '-L', from left to right

2. directories specified by environment variables, such as C_INCLUDE_PATH (for C programs), CPLUS_INCLUDE_PATH (for C++ programs) and LIBRARY_PATH

3. default system directories

In day-to-day usage, directories are usually added to the search paths with the options '-I' and '-L'.

3.2 Shared libraries and static libraries

Although the example program above has been successfully compiled and linked, a final step is needed before being able to load and run the executable file.

If an attempt is made to start the executable directly, the following error will occur on most systems:

```
$ ./a.out
./a.out: error while loading shared libraries:
libgdbm.so.3: cannot open shared object file:
No such file or directory
```
This is because the GDBM package provides a *shared library*. This type of library requires special treatment—it must be loaded from disk before the executable will run.

External libraries are usually provided in two forms: *static libraries* and *shared libraries*. Static libraries are the '.a' files seen earlier. When a program is linked against a static library, the machine code from the object files for any external functions used by the program is copied from the library into the final executable.

Shared libraries are handled with a more advanced form of linking, which makes the executable file smaller. They use the extension '.so', which stands for *shared object*.

An executable file linked against a shared library contains only a small table of the functions it requires, instead of the complete machine code from the object files for the external functions. Before the executable file starts running, the machine code for the external functions is copied into memory from the shared library file on disk by the operating system—a process referred to as *dynamic linking*.

Dynamic linking makes executable files smaller and saves disk space, because one copy of a library can be shared between multiple programs. Most operating systems also provide a virtual memory mechanism which allows one copy of a shared library in physical memory to be used by all running programs, saving memory as well as disk space.

Furthermore, shared libraries make it possible to update a library without recompiling the programs which use it (provided the interface to the library does not change).

Because of these advantages gcc compiles programs to use shared libraries by default on most systems, if they are available. Whenever a static library 'lib*NAME*.a' would be used for linking with the option '-l*NAME*' the compiler first checks for an alternative shared library with the same name and a '.so' extension.

In this case, when the compiler searches for the 'libgdbm' library in the link path, it finds the following two files in the directory '/opt/gdbm-1.8.3/lib':

```
$ cd /opt/gdbm-1.8.3/lib
$ ls libgdbm.*
libgdbm.a  libgdbm.so
```

Consequently, the 'libgdbm.so' shared object file is used in preference to the 'libgdbm.a' static library.

However, when the executable file is started its loader function must find the shared library in order to load it into memory. By default the loader searches for shared libraries only in a predefined set of system directories, such as '/usr/local/lib' and '/usr/lib'. If the library is not located in one of these directories it must be added to the load path.[4]

The simplest way to set the load path is through the environment variable LD_LIBRARY_PATH. For example, the following commands set the load path to '/opt/gdbm-1.8.3/lib' so that 'libgdbm.so' can be found:

```
$ LD_LIBRARY_PATH=/opt/gdbm-1.8.3/lib
$ export LD_LIBRARY_PATH
$ ./a.out
Storing key-value pair... done.
```

The executable now runs successfully, prints its message and creates a DBM file called 'test' containing the key-value pair 'testkey' and 'testvalue'.

---

[4] Note that the directory containing the shared library can, in principle, be stored ("hard-coded") in the executable itself using the linker option '-rpath', but this is not usually done since it creates problems if the library is moved or the executable is copied to another system.

To save typing, the `LD_LIBRARY_PATH` environment variable can be set automatically for each session using the appropriate login file, such as '`.bash_profile`' for the GNU Bash shell.

Several shared library directories can be placed in the load path, as a colon separated list *DIR1*:*DIR2*:*DIR3*:...:*DIRN*. For example, the following command sets the load path to use the '`lib`' directories under '`/opt/gdbm-1.8.3`' and '`/opt/gtk-1.4`':

```
$ LD_LIBRARY_PATH=/opt/gdbm-1.8.3/lib:/opt/gtk-1.4/lib
$ export LD_LIBRARY_PATH
```

If the load path contains existing entries, it can be extended using the syntax `LD_LIBRARY_PATH=`*NEWDIRS*`:$LD_LIBRARY_PATH`. For example, the following command adds the directory '`/opt/gsl-1.5/lib`' to the load path shown above:

```
$ LD_LIBRARY_PATH=/opt/gsl-1.5/lib:$LD_LIBRARY_PATH
$ echo $LD_LIBRARY_PATH
/opt/gsl-1.5/lib:/opt/gdbm-1.8.3/lib:/opt/gtk-1.4/lib
```

It is possible for the system administrator to set the `LD_LIBRARY_PATH` variable for all users, by adding it to a default login script, such as '`/etc/profile`'. On GNU systems, a system-wide path can also be defined in the loader configuration file '`/etc/ld.so.conf`'.

Alternatively, static linking can be forced with the '`-static`' option to gcc to avoid the use of shared libraries:

```
$ gcc -Wall -static -I/opt/gdbm-1.8.3/include/
    -L/opt/gdbm-1.8.3/lib/ dbmain.c -lgdbm
```

This creates an executable linked with the static library '`libgdbm.a`' which can be run without setting the environment variable `LD_LIBRARY_PATH` or putting shared libraries in the default directories:

```
$ ./a.out
Storing key-value pair... done.
```

As noted earlier, it is also possible to link directly with individual library files by specifying the full path to the library on the command line. For example, the following command will link directly with the static library '`libgdbm.a`',

```
$ gcc -Wall -I/opt/gdbm-1.8.3/include
    dbmain.c /opt/gdbm-1.8.3/lib/libgdbm.a
```

and the command below will link with the shared library file '`libgdbm.so`':

```
$ gcc -Wall -I/opt/gdbm-1.8.3/include
    dbmain.c /opt/gdbm-1.8.3/lib/libgdbm.so
```

In the latter case it is still necessary to set the library load path when running the executable.

3.3 C language standards

By default, gcc compiles programs using the GNU dialect of the C
language, referred to as *GNU C*. This dialect incorporates the official
ANSI/ISO standard for the C language with several useful GNU extensions, such as nested functions and variable-size arrays. Most ANSI/ISO
programs will compile under GNU C without changes.

There are several options which control the dialect of C used by gcc.
The most commonly-used options are '-ansi' and '-pedantic'. The specific dialects of the C language for each standard can also be selected with
the '-std' option.

3.3.1 ANSI/ISO

Occasionally a valid ANSI/ISO program may be incompatible with the
extensions in GNU C. To deal with this situation, the compiler option
'-ansi' disables those GNU extensions which are in conflict with the
ANSI/ISO standard. On systems using the GNU C Library (glibc) it
also disables extensions to the C standard library. This allows programs
written for ANSI/ISO C to be compiled without any unwanted effects
from GNU extensions.

For example, here is a valid ANSI/ISO C program which uses a variable
called asm:

```
#include <stdio.h>

int
main (void)
{
   const char asm[] = "6502";
   printf ("the string asm is '%s'\n", asm);
   return 0;
}
```

The variable name asm is valid under the ANSI/ISO standard, but this
program will not compile in GNU C because asm is a GNU C keyword
extension (it allows native assembly instructions to be used in C functions). Consequently, it cannot be used as a variable name without giving
a compilation error:

```
$ gcc -Wall ansi.c
ansi.c: In function 'main':
ansi.c:6: parse error before 'asm'
ansi.c:7: parse error before 'asm'
```

In contrast, using the '-ansi' option disables the asm keyword extension,
and allows the program above to be compiled correctly:

```
$ gcc -Wall -ansi ansi.c
$ ./a.out
the string asm is '6502'
```

For reference, the non-standard keywords and macros defined by the GNU C extensions are asm, inline, typeof, unix and vax. More details can be found in the GCC Reference Manual *"Using GCC"* (see [Further reading], page 111).

The next example shows the effect of the '-ansi' option on systems using the GNU C Library, such as GNU/Linux systems. The program below prints the value of pi, $\pi = 3.14159...$, from the preprocessor definition M_PI in the header file 'math.h':

```
#include <math.h>
#include <stdio.h>

int
main (void)
{
  printf("the value of pi is %f\n", M_PI);
  return 0;
}
```

The constant M_PI is not part of the ANSI/ISO C standard library (it comes from the BSD version of Unix). In this case, the program will not compile with the '-ansi' option:

```
$ gcc -Wall -ansi pi.c
pi.c: In function 'main':
pi.c:7: 'M_PI' undeclared (first use in this function)
pi.c:7: (Each undeclared identifier is reported only once
pi.c:7: for each function it appears in.)
```

The program can be compiled without the '-ansi' option. In this case both the language and library extensions are enabled by default:

```
$ gcc -Wall pi.c
$ ./a.out
the value of pi is 3.141593
```

It is also possible to compile the program using ANSI/ISO C, by enabling only the extensions in the GNU C Library itself. This can be achieved by defining special macros, such as _GNU_SOURCE, which enable extensions in the GNU C Library:[5]

```
$ gcc -Wall -ansi -D_GNU_SOURCE pi.c
$ ./a.out
```

---

[5] The '-D' option for defining macros will be explained in detail in the next chapter.

the value of pi is 3.141593

The GNU C Library provides a number of these macros (referred to as
feature test macros) which allow control over the support for POSIX extensions (_POSIX_C_SOURCE), BSD extensions (_BSD_SOURCE), SVID extensions (_SVID_SOURCE), XOPEN extensions (_XOPEN_SOURCE) and GNU
extensions (_GNU_SOURCE).

The _GNU_SOURCE macro enables all the extensions together, with the
POSIX extensions taking precedence over the others in cases where they
conflict. Further information about feature test macros can be found in
the *GNU C Library Reference Manual* (see [Further reading], page 111).

3.3.2 Strict ANSI/ISO

The command-line option '-pedantic' in combination with '-ansi' will
cause gcc to reject all GNU C extensions, not just those that are incompatible with the ANSI/ISO standard. This helps you to write portable
programs which follow the ANSI/ISO standard.

Here is a program which uses variable-size arrays, a GNU C extension.
The array x[n] is declared with a length specified by the integer variable
n.

```
int
main (int argc, char *argv[])
{
  int i, n = argc;
  double x[n];

  for (i = 0; i < n; i++)
    x[i] = i;

  return 0;
}
```

This program will compile with '-ansi', because support for variable
length arrays does not interfere with the compilation of valid ANSI/ISO
programs—it is a backwards-compatible extension:

```
$ gcc -Wall -ansi gnuarray.c
```

However, compiling with '-ansi -pedantic' reports warnings about vio-
lations of the ANSI/ISO standard:

```
$ gcc -Wall -ansi -pedantic gnuarray.c
gnuarray.c: In function 'main':
gnuarray.c:5: warning: ISO C90 forbids variable-size
  array 'x'
```

Note that an absence of warnings from '-ansi -pedantic' does not guarantee that a program strictly conforms to the ANSI/ISO standard. The standard itself specifies only a limited set of circumstances that should generate diagnostics, and these are what '-ansi -pedantic' reports.

3.3.3 Selecting specific standards

The specific language standard used by GCC can be controlled with the '-std' option. The following C language standards are supported:

'-std=c89' or '-std=iso9899:1990'

> The original ANSI/ISO C language standard (ANSI X3.159-1989, ISO/IEC 9899:1990). GCC incorporates the corrections in the two ISO Technical Corrigenda to the original standard.

'-std=iso9899:199409'

> The ISO C language standard with ISO Amendment 1, published in 1994. This amendment was mainly concerned with internationalization, such as adding support for multibyte characters to the C library.

'-std=c99' or '-std=iso9899:1999'

> The revised ISO C language standard, published in 1999 (ISO/IEC 9899:1999).

The C language standards with GNU extensions can be selected with the options '-std=gnu89' and '-std=gnu99'.

3.4 Warning options in -Wall

As described earlier (see Section 2.1 [Compiling a simple C program], page 7), the warning option '-Wall' enables warnings for many common errors, and should always be used. It combines a large number of other, more specific, warning options which can also be selected individually. Here is a summary of these options:

'-Wcomment' (included in '-Wall')

> This option warns about nested comments. Nested comments typically arise when a section of code containing comments is later *commented out*:

> ```
> /* commented out
> double x = 1.23 ; /* x-position */
> */
> ```

> Nested comments can be a source of confusion—the safe way to "comment out" a section of code containing comments is to surround it with the preprocessor directive #if 0 ... #endif:

```
/* commented out */
#if 0
double x = 1.23 ; /* x-position */
#endif
```

'-Wformat' (included in '-Wall')

This option warns about the incorrect use of format strings in functions such as printf and scanf, where the format specifier does not agree with the type of the corresponding function argument.

'-Wunused' (included in '-Wall')

This option warns about unused variables. When a variable is declared but not used this can be the result of another variable being accidentally substituted in its place. If the variable is genuinely not needed it can be removed from the source code.

'-Wimplicit' (included in '-Wall')

This option warns about any functions that are used without being declared. The most common reason for a function to be used without being declared is forgetting to include a header file.

'-Wreturn-type' (included in '-Wall')

This option warns about functions that are defined without a return type but not declared void. It also catches empty return statements in functions that are not declared void.

For example, the following program does not use an explicit return value:

```
#include <stdio.h>

int
main (void)
{
  printf ("hello world\n");
  return;
}
```

The lack of a return value in the code above could be the result of an accidental omission by the programmer—the value returned by the main function is actually the return value of the printf function (the number of characters printed). To avoid ambiguity, it is preferable to use an explicit value in the return statement, either as a variable or a constant, such as return 0.

The complete set of warning options included in '-Wall' can be found in the GCC Reference Manual "Using GCC" (see [Further reading], page 111). The options included in '-Wall' have the common characteristic that they report constructions which are always wrong, or can easily be rewritten in an unambiguously correct way. This is why they are so useful—any warning produced by '-Wall' can be taken as an indication of a potentially serious problem.

3.5 Additional warning options

GCC provides many other warning options that are not included in '-Wall' but are often useful. Typically these produce warnings for source code which may be technically valid but is very likely to cause problems. The criteria for these options are based on experience of common errors—they are not included in '-Wall' because they only indicate possibly problematic or "suspicious" code.

Since these warnings can be issued for valid code it is not necessary to compile with them all the time. It is more appropriate to use them periodically and review the results, checking for anything unexpected, or to enable them for some programs or files.

'-W'   This is a general option similar to '-Wall' which warns about a selection of common programming errors, such as functions which can return without a value (also known as "falling off the end of the function body"), and comparisons between signed and unsigned values. For example, the following function tests whether an unsigned integer is negative (which is impossible, of course):

```
int
foo (unsigned int x)
{
  if (x < 0)
    return 0;   /* cannot occur */
  else
    return 1;
}
```

Compiling this function with '-Wall' does not produce a warning,

```
$ gcc -Wall -c w.c
```

but does give a warning with '-W':

```
$ gcc -W -c w.c
w.c: In function 'foo':
w.c:4: warning: comparison of unsigned
    expression < 0 is always false
```

In practice, the options '-W' and '-Wall' are normally used together.

'-Wconversion'

This option warns about implicit type conversions that could cause unexpected results, such as conversions between floating-point and

integer types, between signed and unsigned types and between
types of different width (e.g. long and short integers). Conversions
can occur in expressions and assignments, and in calls to functions
if the types of the arguments do not match those specified in the
prototype.

For example, the integer absolute value function int abs(int i)
is easily confused with the corresponding floating-point function
double fabs(double x). This can lead to incorrect results, as
shown in the following program:

```
#include <stdio.h>
#include <stdlib.h>

int
main (void)
{
  double x = -3.14;
  double y = abs(x);   /* should be fabs(x) */
  printf("x = %g |x| = %g\n", x, y);
  return 0;
}
```

Compiling this function with '-Wall' does not produce a warning,

```
$ gcc -Wall wabs.c
$ ./a.out
x = -3.14 |x| = 3   (incorrect)
```

but does give a warning with '-Wconversion':

```
gcc -Wall -Wconversion wabs.c
wabs.c: In function 'main':
wabs.c:8: warning: passing arg 1 of 'abs' as
integer rather than floating due to prototype
```

The '-Wconversion' option also catches errors such as the assignment of a negative value to an unsigned variable, as in the following
code,

```
unsigned int x = -1;
```

This is technically allowed by the ANSI/ISO C standard (with the
negative integer being converted to a positive integer, according to
the machine representation) but could be a simple programming
error. If you need to perform such a conversion you can use an
explicit cast, such as (unsigned int)-1, to avoid any warnings
from this option. On two's-complement machines the cast of -1
gives the maximum number that can be represented by an unsigned
integer.

'-Wshadow'

This option warns about the redeclaration of a variable name in a scope where it has already been declared. This is referred to as variable *shadowing*, and causes confusion about which occurrence of the variable corresponds to which value.

The following function declares a local variable y that shadows the declaration in the body of the function:

```
double
test (double x)
{
  double y = 1.0;
  {
    double y;
    y = x;
  }
  return y;
}
```

This is valid ANSI/ISO C, where the return value is 1. The shadowing of the variable y might make it seem (incorrectly) that the return value is x, when looking at the line y = x (especially in a large and complicated function).

Shadowing can also occur for function names. For example, the following program attempts to define a variable sin which shadows the standard function sin(x).

```
double
sin_series (double x)
{
  /* series expansion for small x */
  double sin = x * (1.0 - x * x / 6.0);
  return sin;
}
```

This error will be detected by the '-Wshadow' option.

'-Wcast-qual'

This option warns about pointers that are cast to remove a type qualifier, such as const. For example, the following function discards the const qualifier from its input argument, allowing it to be overwritten:

```
void
f (const char * str)
{
  char * s = (char *)str;
```

```
        s[0] = '\0';
    }
```

The modification of the original contents of str is a violation of its
const property. This option will warn about the improper cast of
the variable str which allows the string to be modified.

'-Wwrite-strings'

This option implicitly gives all string constants defined in the program a const qualifier, causing a compile-time warning if there is
an attempt to overwrite them. The result of modifying a string
constant is not defined by the ANSI/ISO standard, and the use of
writable string constants is deprecated in GCC.

'-Wtraditional'

This option warns about parts of the code which would be interpreted differently by an ANSI/ISO compiler and a "traditional"
pre-ANSI compiler.[6] When maintaining legacy software it may
be necessary to investigate whether the traditional or ANSI/ISO
interpretation was intended in the original code for warnings generated by this option.

The options above produce diagnostic warning messages, but allow the
compilation to continue and produce an object file or executable. For
large programs it can be desirable to catch all the warnings by stopping
the compilation whenever a warning is generated. The '-Werror' option
changes the default behavior by converting warnings into errors, stopping
the compilation whenever a warning occurs.

3.6 Recommended warning options

The following options are a good choice for finding problems in C and
C++ programs:

```
$ gcc -ansi -pedantic -Wall -W -Wconversion
    -Wshadow -Wcast-qual -Wwrite-strings
```

While this list is not exhaustive, regular use of these options will catch
many common errors.

---

[6] The traditional form of the C language was described in the original C reference manual "The C Programming Language (First Edition)" by Kernighan
and Ritchie.

4 Using the preprocessor

This chapter describes the use of the GNU C preprocessor cpp, which is part of the GCC package. The preprocessor expands macros in source files before they are compiled. It is automatically called whenever GCC processes a C or C++ program.[1]

4.1 Defining macros

The following program demonstrates the most common use of the C preprocessor. It uses the preprocessor conditional #ifdef to check whether a macro is defined:

```
#include <stdio.h>

int
main (void)
{
#ifdef TEST
  printf ("Test mode\n");
#endif
  printf ("Running...\n");
  return 0;
}
```

When the macro is defined, the preprocessor includes the corresponding code up to the closing #endif command. In this example, the macro which is tested is called TEST, and the conditional part of the source code is a printf statement which prints the message "Test mode".

The gcc option '-D*NAME*' defines a preprocessor macro NAME from the command line. If the program above is compiled with the command-line option '-DTEST', the macro TEST will be defined and the resulting executable will print both messages:

```
$ gcc -Wall -DTEST dtest.c
$ ./a.out
Test mode
Running...
```

If the same program is compiled without the '-D' option then the "Test mode" message is omitted from the source code after preprocessing, and the final executable does not include the code for it:

---

[1] In recent versions of GCC the preprocessor is integrated into the compiler, although a separate cpp command is also provided.

```
$ gcc -Wall dtest.c
$ ./a.out
Running...
```

Macros are generally undefined, unless specified on the command line with
the option '-D', or in a source file (or library header file) with #define.
Some macros are automatically defined by the compiler—these typically
use a reserved namespace beginning with a double-underscore prefix '__'.

The complete set of predefined macros can be listed by running the
GNU preprocessor cpp with the option '-dM' on an empty file:

```
$ cpp -dM /dev/null
#define __i386__ 1
#define __i386 1
#define i386 1
#define __unix 1
#define __unix__ 1
#define __ELF__ 1
#define unix 1
.......
```

Note that this list includes a small number of system-specific macros defined by gcc which do not use the double-underscore prefix. These non-
standard macros can be disabled with the '-ansi' option of gcc.

4.2 Macros with values

In addition to being defined, a macro can also be given a value. This value
is inserted into the source code at each point where the macro occurs. The
following program uses a macro NUM, to represent a number which will be
printed:

```
#include <stdio.h>

int
main (void)
{
  printf("Value of NUM is %d\n", NUM);
  return 0;
}
```

Note that macros are not expanded inside strings—only the occurrence of
NUM outside the string is substituted by the preprocessor.

To define a macro with a value, the '-D' command-line option can be
used in the form '-DNAME=VALUE'. For example, the following command
line defines NUM to be 100 when compiling the program above:

```
$ gcc -Wall -DNUM=100 dtestval.c
```

```
$ ./a.out
Value of NUM is 100
```

This example uses a number, but a macro can take values of any form.
Whatever the value of the macro is, it is inserted directly into the source
code at the point where the macro name occurs. For example, the following definition expands the occurrences of NUM to 2+2 during preprocessing:

```
$ gcc -Wall -DNUM="2+2" dtestval.c
$ ./a.out
Value of NUM is 4
```

After the preprocessor has made the substitution NUM ↦ 2+2 this is equivalent to compiling the following program:

```
#include <stdio.h>

int
main (void)
{
    printf("Value of NUM is %d\n", 2+2);
    return 0;
}
```

Note that it is a good idea to surround macros by parentheses whenever they are part of an expression. For example, the following program
uses parentheses to ensure the correct precedence for the multiplication
10*NUM:

```
#include <stdio.h>

int
main (void)
{
    printf ("Ten times NUM is %d\n", 10 * (NUM));
    return 0;
}
```

With these parentheses, it produces the expected result when compiled
with the same command line as above:

```
$ gcc -Wall -DNUM="2+2" dtestmul10.c
$ ./a.out
Ten times NUM is 40
```

Without parentheses, the program would produce the value 22 from the
literal form of the expression 10*2+2 = 22, instead of the desired value
10*(2+2) = 40.

When a macro is defined with '-D' alone, gcc uses a default value of 1.
For example, compiling the original test program with the option '-DNUM'
generates an executable which produces the following output:

```
$ gcc -Wall -DNUM dtestval.c
$ ./a.out
Value of NUM is 1
```

A macro can be defined with an empty value using quotes on the command
line, -DNAME="". Such a macro is still treated as *defined* by conditionals
such as #ifdef, but expands to nothing.

A macro containing quotes can be defined using shell-escaped quote
characters. For example, the command-line option -DMESSAGE='"Hello,
World!"' defines a macro MESSAGE which expands to the sequence of
characters "Hello, World!". The outer shell-quotes '...' protect the
C-quotes of the string "Hello, World!". For an explanation of the different types of quoting and escaping used in the shell see the *"GNU Bash
Reference Manual"*, [Further reading], page 111.

4.3 Preprocessing source files

It is possible to see the effect of the preprocessor on source files directly,
using the '-E' option of gcc. For example, the file below defines and uses
a macro TEST:

```
#define TEST "Hello, World!"
const char str[] = TEST;
```

If this file is called 'test.c' the effect of the preprocessor can be seen with
the following command line:

```
$ gcc -E test.c
# 1 "test.c"

const char str[] = "Hello, World!" ;
```

The '-E' option causes gcc to run the preprocessor, display the expanded
output, and then exit without compiling the resulting source code. The
value of the macro TEST is substituted directly into the output, producing
the sequence of characters const char str[] = "Hello, World!" ;.

The preprocessor also inserts lines recording the source file and line
numbers in the form # *line-number* "*source-file*", to aid in debugging
and allow the compiler to issue error messages referring to this information. These lines do not affect the program itself.

The ability to see the preprocessed source files can be useful for examining the effect of system header files, and finding declarations of system
functions. The following program includes the header file 'stdio.h' to
obtain the declaration of the function printf:

```
#include <stdio.h>

int
```

```
main (void)
{
  printf ("Hello, world!\n");
  return 0;
}
```

It is possible to see the declarations from the included header file by preprocessing the file with gcc -E:

```
$ gcc -E hello.c
```

On a GNU system, this produces output similar to the following:

```
# 1 "hello.c"
# 1 "/usr/include/stdio.h" 1 3

extern FILE *stdin;
extern FILE *stdout;
extern FILE *stderr;

extern int fprintf (FILE * __stream,
                    const char * __format, ...)  ;
extern int printf (const char * __format, ...)  ;
```

  [... additional declarations ...]

```
# 1 "hello.c" 2

int
main (void)
{
  printf ("Hello, world!\n");
  return 0;
}
```

The preprocessed system header files usually generate a lot of output. This can be redirected to a file, or saved more conveniently using the gcc '-save-temps' option:

```
$ gcc -c -save-temps hello.c
```

After running this command, the preprocessed output will be available in the file 'hello.i'. The '-save-temps' option also saves '.s' assembly files and '.o' object files in addition to preprocessed '.i' files.

5 Compiling for debugging

Normally, an executable file does not contain any references to the original program source code, such as variable names or line-numbers—the executable file is simply the sequence of machine code instructions produced by the compiler. This is insufficient for debugging, since there is no easy way to find the cause of an error if the program crashes.

GCC provides the '-g' *debug option* to store additional debugging information in object files and executables. This debugging information allows errors to be traced back from a specific machine instruction to the corresponding line in the original source file. The execution of a program compiled with '-g' can also be followed in a debugger, such as the GNU Debugger gdb (for more information, see *"Debugging with GDB: The GNU Source-Level Debugger"*, [Further reading], page 111). Using a debugger allows the values of variables to be examined while the program is running.

The debug compilation option works by storing the names and source code line-numbers of functions and variables in a *symbol table* in the object file or executable.

5.1 Examining core files

In addition to allowing programs to be run under the debugger, an important benefit of the '-g' option is the ability to examine the cause of a program crash from a "core dump".

When a program exits abnormally (i.e. crashes) the operating system can write out a *core file* (usually named 'core') which contains the in-memory state of the program at the time it crashed. This file is often referred to as a *core dump*.[1] Combined with information from the symbol table produced by '-g', the core dump can be used to find the line where the program stopped, and the values of its variables at that point.

This is useful both during the development of software and after deployment—it allows problems to be investigated when a program has crashed "in the field".

Here is a simple program containing an invalid memory access bug, which we will use to produce a core file:

```
int foo (int *p);

int
```

---

[1] The terminology dates back to the time of magnetic core memory.

```
main (void)
{
  int *p = 0;    /* null pointer */
  return foo (p);
}

int
foo (int *p)
{
  int y = *p;
  return y;
}
```

The program attempts to dereference a null pointer p, which is an invalid operation. On most systems, this will cause a crash.[2]

In order to be able to find the cause of the crash later, we will need to compile the program with the '-g' option:

    $ gcc -Wall -g null.c

Note that a null pointer will only cause a problem at run-time, so the option '-Wall' does not produce any warnings.

Running the executable file on an x86 GNU/Linux system will cause the operating system to terminate the program abnormally:

    $ ./a.out
    Segmentation fault (core dumped)

Whenever the error message 'core dumped' is displayed, the operating system should produce a file called 'core' in the current directory.[3] This core file contains a complete copy of the pages of memory used by the program at the time it was terminated. Incidentally, the term *segmentation fault* refers to the fact that the program tried to access a restricted memory "segment" outside the area of memory which had been allocated to it.

Some systems are configured not to write core files by default, since the files can be large and rapidly fill up the available disk space on a system. In the *GNU Bash* shell the command ulimit -c controls the maximum size of core files. If the size limit is zero, no core files are produced. The current size limit can be shown by typing the following command:

---

[2] Historically, a null pointer corresponded to memory location 0, which is typically restricted to the operating system kernel. In practice this is not always how a null pointer works, but the result is usually the same.

[3] Some systems, such as FreeBSD and Solaris, can also be configured to write core files in specific directories, e.g. '/var/coredumps/', using the sysctl or coreadm commands.

```
$ ulimit -c
0
```

If the result is zero, as shown above, then it can be increased with the following command to allow core files of any size to be written:[4]

```
$ ulimit -c unlimited
```

Note that this setting only applies to the current shell. To set the limit for future sessions the command should be placed in an appropriate login file, such as '.bash_profile' for the GNU Bash shell.

Core files can be loaded into the GNU Debugger gdb with the following command:

```
$ gdb EXECUTABLE-FILE CORE-FILE
```

Note that both the original executable file and the core file are required for debugging—it is not possible to debug a core file without the corresponding executable. In this example, we can load the executable and core file with the command:

```
$ gdb a.out core
```

The debugger immediately begins printing diagnostic information, and shows a listing of the line where the program crashed (line 13):

```
$ gdb a.out core
Core was generated by './a.out'.
Program terminated with signal 11, Segmentation fault.
Reading symbols from /lib/libc.so.6...done.
Loaded symbols for /lib/libc.so.6
Reading symbols from /lib/ld-linux.so.2...done.
Loaded symbols for /lib/ld-linux.so.2
#0  0x080483ed in foo (p=0x0) at null.c:13
13              int y = *p;
(gdb)
```

The final line (gdb) is the GNU Debugger prompt—it indicates that further commands can be entered at this point.

To investigate the cause of the crash, we display the value of the pointer p using the debugger print command:

```
(gdb) print p
$1 = (int *) 0x0
```

This shows that p is a null pointer (0x0) of type 'int *', so we know that dereferencing it with the expression *p in this line has caused the crash.

---

[4] This example uses the ulimit command in the GNU Bash shell. On other systems the usage of the ulimit command may vary, or have a different name (the tcsh shell uses the limit command instead). The size limit for core files can also be set to a specific value in kilobytes.

5.2 Displaying a backtrace

The debugger can also show the function calls and arguments up to the
current point of execution—this is called a *stack backtrace* and is displayed with the command backtrace:

```
(gdb) backtrace
#0  0x080483ed in foo (p=0x0) at null.c:13
#1  0x080483d9 in main () at null.c:7
```

In this case, the backtrace shows that the crash occurred at line 13 after
the function foo was called from main with an argument of p=0x0 at line
7 in 'null.c'. It is possible to move to different levels in the stack trace,
and examine their variables, using the debugger commands up and down.

5.3 Setting a breakpoint

A *breakpoint* stops the execution of a program and returns control to
the debugger, where its variables and memory can be examined before
continuing. Breakpoints can be set for specific functions, lines or memory
locations with the break command.

To set a breakpoint on a specific function, use the command break
function-name. For example, the following command sets a breakpoint
at the start of the main function in the program above:

```
$ gdb a.out
(gdb) break main
Breakpoint 1 at 0x80483c6: file null.c, line 6.
```

The debugger will now take control of the program when the function
main is called. Since the main function is the first function to be executed
in a C program the program will stop immediately when it is run:

```
(gdb) run
Starting program: a.out
Breakpoint 1, main () at null.c:6
6            int *p = 0;    /* null pointer */
(gdb)
```

The display shows the line that will be executed next (the line number is
shown on the left). The breakpoint stops the program *before* the line is
executed, so at this stage the pointer p is undefined and has not yet been
set to zero.

5.4 Stepping through the program

To move forward and execute the line displayed above, use the command
step:

```
(gdb) step
7                return foo (p);
```

After executing line 6, the debugger displays the next line to be executed.
The pointer p will now have been set to zero (null):

```
(gdb) print p
$1 = (int *) 0x0
```

The command step will follow the execution of the program interactively
through any functions that are called in the current line. If you want to
move forward without tracing these calls, use the command next instead.

5.5 Modifying variables

To temporarily fix the null pointer bug discovered above, we can change
the value of p in the running program using the set variable command.

Variables can be set to a specific value, or to the result of an expression,
which may include function calls. This powerful feature allows functions
in a program to be tested interactively through the debugger.

In this case we will interactively allocate some memory for the pointer
p using the function malloc, storing the value 255 in the resulting location:

```
(gdb) set variable p = malloc(sizeof(int))
(gdb) print p
$2 = (int *) 0x40013f98       (address allocated by malloc)
(gdb) set variable *p = 255
(gdb) print *p
$3 = 255
```

If we now continue stepping through the program with the new value of
p the previous segmentation fault will not occur:

```
(gdb) step
foo (p=0x40013f98) at null.c:13
13            int y = *p;
(gdb) step
14            return y;
```

5.6 Continuing execution

The command finish continues execution up to the end of the current
function, displaying the return value:

```
(gdb) finish
Run till exit from #0  0x08048400 in foo (p=0x40013f98)
at null.c:15
0x080483d9 in main () at null.c:7
7                return foo (p);
```

```
Value returned is $13 = 255
```

To continue execution until the program exits (or hits the next breakpoint) use the command continue,

```
(gdb) continue
Continuing.
Program exited with code 0377.
```

Note that the exit code is shown in octal (0377 base 8 = 255 in base 10).

5.7 More information

For simplicity, the examples in this chapter demonstrate how to use gdb on the command-line. There are more powerful ways to debug a program interactively using tools such as Emacs GDB mode (*M-x gdb*), DDD or INSIGHT, graphical interfaces to gdb. Links to these programs can be found on the publisher's webpage for this book.[5]

A complete description of all the commands available in gdb can be found in the manual "*Debugging with GDB: The GNU Source-Level Debugger*" (see [Further reading], page 111).

---

[5] http://www.network-theory.co.uk/gcc/intro/

6 Compiling with optimization

GCC is an *optimizing* compiler. It provides a wide range of options which aim to increase the speed, or reduce the size, of the executable files it generates.

Optimization is a complex process. For each high-level command in the source code there are usually many possible combinations of machine instructions that can be used to achieve the appropriate final result. The compiler must consider these possibilities and choose among them.

In general, different code must be generated for different processors, as they use incompatible assembly and machine languages. Each type of processor also has its own characteristics—some CPUs provide a large number of *registers* for holding intermediate results of calculations, while others must store and fetch intermediate results from memory. Appropriate code must be generated in each case.

Furthermore, different amounts of time are needed for different instructions, depending on how they are ordered. GCC takes all these factors into account and tries to produce the fastest executable for a given system when compiling with optimization.

6.1 Source-level optimization

The first form of optimization used by GCC occurs at the source-code level, and does not require any knowledge of the machine instructions. There are many source-level optimization techniques—this section describes two common types: *common subexpression elimination* and *function inlining*.

6.1.1 Common subexpression elimination

One method of source-level optimization which is easy to understand involves computing an expression in the source code with fewer instructions, by reusing already-computed results. For example, the following assignment:

```
x = cos(v)*(1+sin(u/2)) + sin(w)*(1-sin(u/2))
```

can be rewritten with a temporary variable t to eliminate an unnecessary extra evaluation of the term sin(u/2):

```
t = sin(u/2)
x = cos(v)*(1+t) + sin(w)*(1-t)
```

This rewriting is called *common subexpression elimination* (CSE), and is performed automatically when optimization is turned on.[1] Common subexpression elimination is powerful, because it simultaneously increases the speed and reduces the size of the code.

6.1.2 Function inlining

Another type of source-level optimization, called *function inlining*, increases the efficiency of frequently-called functions.

Whenever a function is used, a certain amount of extra time is required for the CPU to carry out the call: it must store the function arguments in the appropriate registers and memory locations, jump to the start of the function (bringing the appropriate virtual memory pages into physical memory or the CPU cache if necessary), begin executing the code, and then return to the original point of execution when the function call is complete. This additional work is referred to as *function-call overhead*. Function inlining eliminates this overhead by replacing calls to a function by the code of the function itself (known as placing the code *in-line*).

In most cases, function-call overhead is a negligible fraction of the total run-time of a program. It can become significant only when there are functions which contain relatively few instructions, and these functions account for a substantial fraction of the run-time—in this case the overhead then becomes a large proportion of the total run-time.

Inlining is always favorable if there is only one point of invocation of a function. It is also unconditionally better if the invocation of a function requires more instructions (memory) than moving the body of the function in-line. This is a common situation for simple accessor functions in C++, which can benefit greatly from inlining. Moreover, inlining may facilitate further optimizations, such as common subexpression elimination, by merging several separate functions into a single large function.

The following function sq(x) is a typical example of a function that would benefit from being inlined. It computes x^2, the square of its argument x:

```
double
sq (double x)
{
  return x * x;
}
```

---

[1] Temporary values introduced by the compiler during common subexpression elimination are only used internally, and do not affect real variables. The name of the temporary variable 't' shown above is only used as an illustration.

This function is small, so the overhead of calling it is comparable to the time taken to execute the single multiplication carried out by the function itself. If this function is used inside a loop, such as the one below, then the function-call overhead would become substantial:

```
for (i = 0; i < 1000000; i++)
  {
    sum += sq (i + 0.5);
  }
```

Optimization with inlining replaces the inner loop of the program with the body of the function, giving the following code:

```
for (i = 0; i < 1000000; i++)
  {
    double t = (i + 0.5);   /* temporary variable */
    sum += t * t;
  }
```

Eliminating the function call and performing the multiplication *in-line* allows the loop to run with maximum efficiency.

GCC selects functions for inlining using a number of heuristics, such as the function being suitably small. As an optimization, inlining is carried out only within each object file. The `inline` keyword can be used to request explicitly that a specific function should be inlined wherever possible, including its use in other files.[2] The GCC Reference Manual "*Using GCC*" provides full details of the `inline` keyword, and its use with the `static` and `extern` qualifiers to control the linkage of explicitly inlined functions (see [Further reading], page 111).

6.2 Speed-space tradeoffs

While some forms of optimization, such as common subexpression elimination, are able to increase the speed and reduce the size of a program simultaneously, other types of optimization produce faster code at the expense of increasing the size of the executable. This choice between speed and memory is referred to as a *speed-space tradeoff*. Optimizations with a speed-space tradeoff can also be used in reverse to make an executable smaller, at the expense of making it run slower.

6.2.1 Loop unrolling

A prime example of an optimization with a speed-space tradeoff is *loop unrolling*. This form of optimization increases the speed of loops by elim-

---

[2] In this case, the definition of the inline function must be made available to the other files (e.g. in a header file).

inating the "end of loop" condition on each iteration. For example, the following loop from 0 to 7 tests the condition i < 8 on each iteration:

```
for (i = 0; i < 8; i++)
  {
    y[i] = i;
  }
```

At the end of the loop, this test will have been performed 9 times, and a large fraction of the run time will have been spent checking it.

A more efficient way to write the same code is simply to *unroll the loop* and execute the assignments directly:

```
y[0] = 0;
y[1] = 1;
y[2] = 2;
y[3] = 3;
y[4] = 4;
y[5] = 5;
y[6] = 6;
y[7] = 7;
```

This form of the code does not require any tests, and executes at maximum speed. Since each assignment is independent, it also allows the compiler to use parallelism on processors that support it. Loop unrolling is an optimization that increases the speed of the resulting executable but also generally increases its size (unless the loop is very short, with only one or two iterations, for example).

Loop unrolling is also possible when the upper bound of the loop is unknown, provided the start and end conditions are handled correctly. For example, the same loop with an arbitrary upper bound,

```
for (i = 0; i < n; i++)
  {
    y[i] = i;
  }
```

can be rewritten by the compiler as follows:

```
for (i = 0; i < (n % 2); i++)
  {
    y[i] = i;
  }

for ( ; i + 1 < n; i += 2) /* no initializer */
  {
    y[i] = i;
    y[i+1] = i+1;
  }
```

The first loop handles the case i = 0 when n is odd, and the second loop handles all the remaining iterations. Note that the second loop does not use an initializer in the first argument of the for statement, since it continues where the first loop finishes. The assignments in the second loop can be parallelized, and the overall number of tests is reduced by a factor of 2 (approximately). Higher factors can be achieved by unrolling more assignments inside the loop, at the cost of greater code size.

6.3 Scheduling

The lowest level of optimization is *scheduling*, in which the compiler determines the best ordering of individual instructions. Most CPUs allow one or more new instructions to start executing before others have finished. Many CPUs also support *pipelining*, where multiple instructions execute in parallel on the same CPU.

When scheduling is enabled, instructions must be arranged so that their results become available to later instructions at the right time, and to allow for maximum parallel execution. Scheduling improves the speed of an executable without increasing its size, but requires additional memory and time in the compilation process itself (due to its complexity).

6.4 Optimization levels

In order to control compilation-time and compiler memory usage, and the trade-offs between speed and space for the resulting executable, GCC provides a range of general optimization levels, numbered from 0–3, as well as individual options for specific types of optimization.

An optimization level is chosen with the command line option '-O*LEVEL*', where *LEVEL* is a number from 0 to 3. The effects of the different optimization levels are described below:

'-O0' or no '-O' option (default)

> At this optimization level GCC does not perform any optimization and compiles the source code in the most straightforward way possible. Each command in the source code is converted directly to the corresponding instructions in the executable file, without rearrangement. This is the best option to use when debugging a program and is the default if no optimization level option is specified.

'-O1' or '-O'

> This level turns on the most common forms of optimization that do not require any speed-space tradeoffs. With this option the resulting executables should be smaller and faster than with '-O0'.

The more expensive optimizations, such as instruction scheduling, are not used at this level.

Compiling with the option '-O1' can often take less time than compiling with '-O0', due to the reduced amounts of data that need to be processed after simple optimizations.

'-O2' This option turns on further optimizations, in addition to those used by '-O1'. These additional optimizations include instruction scheduling. Only optimizations that do not require any speed-space tradeoffs are used, so the executable should not increase in size. The compiler will take longer to compile programs and require more memory than with '-O1'. This option is generally the best choice for deployment of a program, because it provides maximum optimization without increasing the executable size. It is the default optimization level for releases of GNU packages.

'-O3' This option turns on more expensive optimizations, such as function inlining, in addition to all the optimizations of the lower levels '-O2' and '-O1'. The '-O3' optimization level may increase the speed of the resulting executable, but can also increase its size. Under some circumstances where these optimizations are not favorable, this option might actually make a program slower.

'-funroll-loops'
       This option turns on loop-unrolling, and is independent of the other optimization options. It will increase the size of an executable. Whether or not this option produces a beneficial result has to be examined on a case-by-case basis.

'-Os' This option selects optimizations which reduce the size of an executable. The aim of this option is to produce the smallest possible executable, for systems constrained by memory or disk space. In some cases a smaller executable will also run faster, due to better cache usage.

It is important to remember that the benefit of optimization at the highest levels must be weighed against the cost. The cost of optimization includes greater complexity in debugging, and increased time and memory requirements during compilation. For most purposes it is satisfactory to use '-O0' for debugging, and '-O2' for development and deployment.

6.5 Examples

The following program will be used to demonstrate the effects of different optimization levels:

```
#include <stdio.h>

double
powern (double d, unsigned n)
{
  double x = 1.0;
  unsigned j;

  for (j = 1; j <= n; j++)
    x *= d;

  return x;
}

int
main (void)
{
  double sum = 0.0;
  unsigned i;

  for (i = 1; i <= 100000000; i++)
    {
      sum += powern (i, i % 5);
    }

  printf ("sum = %g\n", sum);
  return 0;
}
```

The main program contains a loop calling the powern function. This function computes the n-th power of a floating point number by repeated multiplication—it has been chosen because it is suitable for both inlining and loop-unrolling. The run-time of the program can be measured using the time command in the GNU Bash shell.

Here are some results for the program above, compiled on a 566 MHz Intel Celeron with 16 KB L1-cache and 128 KB L2-cache, using GCC 3.3.1 on a GNU/Linux system:

```
$ gcc -Wall -O0 test.c -lm
$ time ./a.out
real    0m13.388s
user    0m13.370s
sys     0m0.010s

$ gcc -Wall -O1 test.c -lm
```

```
$ time ./a.out
real    0m10.030s
user    0m10.030s
sys     0m0.000s

$ gcc -Wall -O2 test.c -lm
$ time ./a.out
real    0m8.388s
user    0m8.380s
sys     0m0.000s

$ gcc -Wall -O3 test.c -lm
$ time ./a.out
real    0m6.742s
user    0m6.730s
sys     0m0.000s

$ gcc -Wall -O3 -funroll-loops test.c -lm
$ time ./a.out
real    0m5.412s
user    0m5.390s
sys     0m0.000s
```

The relevant entry in the output for comparing the speed of the resulting executables is the 'user' time, which gives the actual CPU time spent running the process. The other rows, 'real' and 'sys', record the total real time for the process to run (including times where other processes were using the CPU) and the time spent waiting for operating system calls. Although only one run is shown for each case above, the benchmarks were executed several times to confirm the results.

From the results it can be seen in this case that increasing the optimization level with '-O1', '-O2' and '-O3' produces an increasing speedup, relative to the unoptimized code compiled with '-O0'. The additional option '-funroll-loops' produces a further speedup. The speed of the program is more than doubled overall, when going from unoptimized code to the highest level of optimization.

Note that for a small program such as this there can be considerable variation between systems and compiler versions. For example, on a Mobile 2.0 GHz Intel Pentium 4M system the trend of the results using the same version of GCC is similar except that the performance with '-O2' is slightly worse than with '-O1'. This illustrates an important point: optimizations may not necessarily make a program faster in every case.

6.6 Optimization and debugging

With GCC it is possible to use optimization in combination with the debugging option '-g'. Many other compilers do not allow this.

When using debugging and optimization together, the internal rearrangements carried out by the optimizer can make it difficult to see what is going on when examining an optimized program in the debugger. For example, temporary variables are often eliminated, and the ordering of statements may be changed.

However, when a program crashes unexpectedly, any debugging information is better than none—so the use of '-g' is recommended for optimized programs, both for development and deployment. The debugging option '-g' is enabled by default for releases of GNU packages, together with the optimization option '-O2'.

6.7 Optimization and compiler warnings

When optimization is turned on, GCC can produce additional warnings that do not appear when compiling without optimization.

As part of the optimization process, the compiler examines the use of all variables and their initial values—this is referred to as *data-flow analysis*. It forms the basis for other optimization strategies, such as instruction scheduling. A side-effect of data-flow analysis is that the compiler can detect the use of uninitialized variables.

The '-Wuninitialized' option (which is included in '-Wall') warns about variables that are read without being initialized. It only works when the program is compiled with optimization, so that data-flow analysis is enabled. The following function contains an example of such a variable:

```
int
sign (int x)
{
  int s;

  if (x > 0)
    s = 1;
  else if (x < 0)
    s = -1;

  return s;
}
```

The function works correctly for most arguments, but has a bug when x is zero—in this case the return value of the variable s will be undefined.

Compiling the program with the '-Wall' option alone does not produce any warnings, because data-flow analysis is not carried out without optimization:

```
$ gcc -Wall -c uninit.c
```

To produce a warning, the program must be compiled with '-Wall' and optimization simultaneously. In practice, the optimization level '-O2' is needed to give good warnings:

```
$ gcc -Wall -O2 -c uninit.c
uninit.c: In function 'sign':
uninit.c:4: warning: 's' might be used uninitialized
    in this function
```

This correctly detects the possibility of the variable s being used without being defined.

Note that while GCC will usually find most uninitialized variables, it does so using heuristics which will occasionally miss some complicated cases or falsely warn about others. In the latter situation, it is often possible to rewrite the relevant lines in a simpler way that removes the warning and improves the readability of the source code.

7 Compiling a C++ program

This chapter describes how to use GCC to compile programs written in C++, and the command-line options specific to that language.

The GNU C++ compiler provided by GCC is a true C++ compiler—it compiles C++ source code directly into assembly language. Some other C++ "compilers" are translators which convert C++ programs into C, and then compile the resulting C program using an existing C compiler. A true C++ compiler, such as GCC, is able to provide better support for error reporting, debugging and optimization.

7.1 Compiling a simple C++ program

The procedure for compiling a C++ program is the same as for a C program, but uses the command g++ instead of gcc. Both compilers are part of the GNU Compiler Collection.

To demonstrate the use of g++, here is a version of the *Hello World* program written in C++:

```
#include <iostream>

int
main ()
{
  std::cout << "Hello, world!\n";
  return 0;
}
```

The program can be compiled with the following command line:

```
$ g++ -Wall hello.cc -o hello
```

The C++ frontend of GCC uses many of the same the same options as the C compiler gcc. It also supports some additional options for controlling C++ language features, which will be described in this chapter. Note that C++ source code should be given one of the valid C++ file extensions '.cc', '.cpp', '.cxx' or '.C' rather than the '.c' extension used for C programs.

The resulting executable can be run in exactly same way as the C version, simply by typing its filename:

```
$ ./hello
Hello, world!
```

The executable produces the same output as the C version of the program, using std::cout instead of the C printf function. All the options used in the gcc commands in previous chapters apply to g++ without change, as do the procedures for compiling and linking files and libraries (using g++

instead of gcc, of course). One natural difference is that the '-ansi' option requests compliance with the C++ standard, instead of the C standard, when used with g++.

Note that programs using C++ object files must always be linked with g++, in order to supply the appropriate C++ libraries. Attempting to link a C++ object file with the C compiler gcc will cause "undefined reference" errors for C++ standard library functions:

```
$ g++ -Wall -c hello.cc
$ gcc hello.o        (should use g++)
hello.o: In function 'main':
hello.o(.text+0x1b): undefined reference to 'std::cout'
.....
hello.o(.eh_frame+0x11):
    undefined reference to '__gxx_personality_v0'
```

Undefined references to internal run-time library functions, such as __gxx_personality_v0, are also a symptom of linking C++ object files with gcc instead of g++. Linking the same object file with g++ supplies all the necessary C++ libraries and will produce a working executable:

```
$ g++ hello.o
$ ./a.out
Hello, world!
```

A point that sometimes causes confusion is that gcc will actually compile C++ source code when it detects a C++ file extension, but cannot then link the resulting object files.

```
$ gcc -Wall -c hello.cc    (succeeds, even for C++)
$ gcc hello.o
hello.o: In function 'main':
hello.o(.text+0x1b): undefined reference to 'std::cout'
```

To avoid this problem, use g++ consistently for C++ programs and gcc for C programs.

7.2 C++ compilation options

Most GCC options can be used for both C and C++ programs, but there are also a few options which are specific to each language. This section describes some of the additional options, and enhancements to existing options, that are available in g++.

'-Wall' and '-W'

> When compiling with g++, the options '-Wall' and '-W' include extra warnings specific to C++ (the warnings relate to member functions and virtual classes). The use of these options is always recommended while developing a program.

'-fno-default-inline'

> This option disables the default inlining of member functions defined in the bodies of C++ classes. GCC normally inlines all such functions when optimization is turned on, even if they do not explicitly use the `inline` keyword. Select this option if you prefer to control inlining yourself, or want to set a breakpoint on member functions that would otherwise be inlined (since it is not possible to set a breakpoint on an inlined function).

'-Weffc++'

> This option warns about C++ code which breaks some of the programming guidelines given in the books *"Effective C++"* and *"More Effective C++"* by Scott Meyers. For example, a warning will be given if a class which uses dynamically allocated memory does not define a copy constructor and an assignment operator. Note that the standard library header files do not follow these guidelines, so you may wish to use this option as an occasional test for possible problems in your own code rather than compiling with it all the time.

'-Wold-style-cast'

> This option highlights any uses of C-style casts in C++ programs. The C++ language provides the keywords `static_cast`, `dynamic_cast`, `reinterpret_cast` and `const_cast` for handling casts and these are often preferable (although C-style casts are still allowed).

7.3 Using the C++ standard library

An implementation of the C++ standard library is provided as a part of GCC. The following program uses the standard library `string` class to reimplement the *Hello World* program:

```
#include <string>
#include <iostream>

using namespace std;

int
main ()
{
  string s1 = "Hello,";
  string s2 = "World!";
  cout << s1 + " " + s2 << '\n';
  return 0;
}
```

The program can be compiled and run using the same commands as above:

```
$ g++ -Wall hellostr.cc
$ ./a.out
Hello, World!
```

Note that in accordance with the C++ standard, the header files for the C++ library itself do not use a file extension. The classes in the library are also defined in the std namespace, so the directive using namespace std is needed to access them, unless the prefix std:: is used throughout (as in the previous section).

7.4 Templates

Templates provide the ability to define C++ classes which support *generic programming* techniques. Templates can be considered as a powerful kind of macro facility. When a templated class or function is used with a specific class or type, such as float or int, the corresponding template code is compiled with that type substituted in the appropriate places.

7.4.1 Using C++ standard library templates

The C++ standard library 'libstdc++' supplied with GCC provides a wide range of generic container classes such as lists and queues, in addition to generic algorithms such as sorting. These classes were originally part of the Standard Template Library (STL), which was a separate package, but are now included in the C++ standard library itself.

The following program demonstrates the use of the template library by creating a list of strings with the template list<string>:

```
#include <list>
#include <string>
#include <iostream>

using namespace std;

int
main ()
{
  list<string> list;
  list.push_back("Hello");
  list.push_back("World");
  cout << "List size = " << list.size() << '\n';
  return 0;
}
```

No special options are needed to use the template classes in the standard library; the command-line options for compiling this program are the same as before:

```
$ g++ -Wall string.cc
$ ./a.out
List size = 2
```

Note that the executables created by g++ using the C++ standard library will be linked to the shared library 'libstdc++', which is supplied as part of the default GCC installation. There are several versions of this library—if you distribute executables using the C++ standard library you need to ensure that the recipient has a compatible version of 'libstdc++', or link your program statically using the command-line option '-static'.

7.4.2 Providing your own templates

In addition to the template classes provided by the C++ standard library you can define your own templates. The recommended way to use templates with g++ is to follow the *inclusion compilation model*, where template definitions are placed in header files. This is the method used by the C++ standard library supplied with GCC itself. The header files can then be included with '#include' in each source file where they are needed.

For example, the following template file creates a simple Buffer<T> class which represents a circular buffer holding objects of type T.

```
#ifndef BUFFER_H
#define BUFFER_H

template <class T>
class Buffer
{
public:
  Buffer (unsigned int n);
  void insert (const T & x);
  T get (unsigned int k) const;
private:
  unsigned int i;
  unsigned int size;
  T *pT;
};

template <class T>
Buffer<T>::Buffer (unsigned int n)
{
  i = 0;
```

```
    size = n;
    pT = new T[n];
};

template <class T>
void
Buffer<T>::insert (const T & x)
{
    i = (i + 1) % size;
    pT[i] = x;
};

template <class T>
T
Buffer<T>::get (unsigned int k) const
{
    return pT[(i + (size - k)) % size];
};

#endif /* BUFFER_H */
```

The file contains both the declaration of the class and the definitions of
the member functions. This class is only given for demonstration purposes
and should not be considered an example of good programming. Note the
use of *include guards*, which test for the presence of the macro BUFFER_H,
ensuring that the definitions in the header file are only parsed once if the
file is included multiple times in the same context.

The program below uses the templated Buffer class to create a buffer
of size 10, storing the floating point values 0.25 and 1.0 in the buffer:

```
#include <iostream>
#include "buffer.h"

using namespace std;

int
main ()
{
    Buffer<float> f(10);
    f.insert (0.25);
    f.insert (1.0 + f.get(0));
    cout << "stored value = " << f.get(0) << '\n';
    return 0;
}
```

The definitions for the template class and its functions are included in the source file for the program with '#include "buffer.h"' before they are used. The program can then be compiled using the following command line:

```
$ g++ -Wall tprog.cc
$ ./a.out
stored value = 1.25
```

At the points where the template functions are used in the source file, g++ compiles the appropriate definition from the header file and places the compiled function in the corresponding object file.

If a template function is used several times in a program it will be stored in more than one object file. The GNU Linker ensures that only one copy is placed in the final executable. Other linkers may report *"multiply defined symbol"* errors when they encounter more than one copy of a template function—a method of working with these linkers is described below.

7.4.3 Explicit template instantiation

To achieve complete control over the compilation of templates with g++ it is possible to require explicit instantiation of each occurrence of a template, using the option '-fno-implicit-templates'. This method is not needed when using the GNU Linker—it is an alternative provided for systems with linkers which cannot eliminate duplicate definitions of template functions in object files.

In this approach, template functions are no longer compiled at the point where they are used, as a result of the '-fno-implicit-templates' option. Instead, the compiler looks for an explicit instantiation of the template using the template keyword with a specific type to force its compilation (this is a GNU extension to the standard behavior). These instantiations are typically placed in a separate source file, which is then compiled to make an object file containing all the template functions required by a program. This ensures that each template appears in only one object file, and is compatible with linkers which cannot eliminate duplicate definitions in object files.

For example, the following file 'templates.cc' contains an explicit instantiation of the Buffer<float> class used by the program 'tprog.cc' given above:

```
#include "buffer.h"
template class Buffer<float>;
```

The whole program can be compiled and linked using explicit instantiation with the following commands:

```
$ g++ -Wall -fno-implicit-templates -c tprog.cc
$ g++ -Wall -fno-implicit-templates -c templates.cc
$ g++ tprog.o templates.o
$ ./a.out
stored value = 1.25
```

The object code for all the template functions is contained in the
file 'templates.o'. There is no object code for template functions in
'tprog.o' when it is compiled with the '-fno-implicit-templates' option.

If the program is modified to use additional types, then further explicit
instantiations can be added to the file 'templates.cc'. For example, the
following code adds instantiations for Buffer objects containing double
and int values:

```
#include "buffer.h"
template class Buffer<float>;
template class Buffer<double>;
template class Buffer<int>;
```

The disadvantage of explicit instantiation is that it is necessary to know
which template types are needed by the program. For a complicated program this may be difficult to determine in advance. Any missing template
instantiations can be determined at link time, however, and added to the
list of explicit instantiations, by noting which functions are undefined.

Explicit instantiation can also be used to make libraries of precompiled
template functions, by creating an object file containing all the required
instantiations of a template function (as in the file 'templates.cc' above).
For example, the object file created from the template instantiations above
contains the machine code needed for Buffer classes with 'float', 'double'
and 'int' types, and could be distributed in a library.

7.4.4 The export keyword

At the time of writing, GCC does not support the new C++ export keyword (GCC 3.4.4).

This keyword was proposed as a way of separating the interface of
templates from their implementation. However it adds its own complexity
to the linking process, which can detract from any advantages in practice.

The export keyword is not widely used, and most other compilers do
not support it either. The inclusion compilation model described earlier
is recommended as the simplest and most portable way to use templates.

8 Platform-specific options

GCC provides a range of platform-specific options for different types of CPUs. These options control features such as hardware floating-point modes, and the use of special instructions for different CPUs. They can be selected with the '-m' option on the command line, and work with all the GCC language frontends, such as gcc and g++.

The following sections describe some of the options available for common platforms. A complete list of all platform-specific options can be found in the GCC Reference Manual, "*Using GCC*" (see [Further reading], page 111). Support for new processors is added to GCC as they become available, therefore some of the options described in this chapter may not be found in older versions of GCC.

8.1 Intel and AMD x86 options

The features of the widely used Intel and AMD x86 families of processors (386, 486, Pentium, etc) can be controlled with GCC platform-specific options.

On these platforms, GCC produces executable code which is compatible with all the processors in the x86 family by default—going all the way back to the 386. However, it is also possible to compile for a specific processor to obtain better performance.[1]

For example, recent versions of GCC have specific support for newer processors such as the Pentium 4 and AMD Athlon. These can be selected with the following option for the Pentium 4,

    $ gcc -Wall -march=pentium4 hello.c
and for the Athlon:

    $ gcc -Wall -march=athlon hello.c
A complete list of supported CPU types can be found in the GCC Reference Manual.

Code produced with a specific '-march=*CPU*' option will be faster but will not run on other processors in the x86 family. If you plan to distribute executable files for general use on Intel and AMD processors they should be compiled without any '-march' options.

As an alternative, the '-mcpu=*CPU*' option provides a compromise between speed and portability—it generates code that is tuned for a specific processor, in terms of instruction scheduling, but does not use any in-

---

[1] Also referred to as "targeting" a specific processor.

structions which are not available on other CPUs in the x86 family.[2] The resulting code will be compatible with all the CPUs, and have a speed advantage on the CPU specified by '-mcpu'. The executables generated by '-mcpu' cannot achieve the same performance as '-march', but may be more convenient in practice.

8.1.1 x86 extensions

GCC can take advantage of the additional instructions in the MMX, SSE, SSE2, SSE3 and 3dnow extensions of recent Intel and AMD processors. The options '-mmmx', '-msse', '-msse2', '-msse3' and '-m3dnow' enable the use of these extra instructions, allowing multiple words of data to be processed in parallel. The resulting executables will only run on processors supporting the appropriate extensions—on other systems they will crash with an Illegal instruction error (or similar).[3]

The option '-mfpmath=sse' instructs GCC to use the SSE extensions for floating-point arithmetic where possible. For this option to take effect, the SSE or SSE2 extensions must first be enabled with '-msse' or '-msse2'.

Note that the plain SSE extensions only support single precision operations—double precision arithmetic is part of SSE2. Since most C and C++ programs declare floating-point variables as double rather than float, the combined options -msse2 -mfpmath=sse are usually needed. On 64-bit processors these options are enabled by default.

8.1.2 x86 64-bit processors

AMD has enhanced the 32-bit x86 instruction set to a 64-bit instruction set called x86-64, which is implemented in their AMD64 processors.[4] On AMD64 systems GCC generates 64-bit code by default. The option '-m32' allows 32-bit code to be generated instead.

The AMD64 processor has several different memory models for programs running in 64-bit mode. The default model is the small code model, which allows code and data up to 2 GB in size. The medium code model allows unlimited data sizes and can be selected with '-mcmodel=medium'. There is also a large code model, which supports an unlimited code size in addition to unlimited data size. It is not currently implemented in GCC

---

[2] In recent versions of GCC this option has been renamed to '-mtune'. The older form '-mcpu' will continue to work.

[3] On GNU/Linux systems, the command cat /proc/cpuinfo will display information about the CPU.

[4] Intel has added support for this instruction set as the "Intel 64-bit enhancements" on their Xeon CPUs.

since the medium code model is sufficient for all practical purposes—executables with sizes greater than 2 GB are not encountered in practice.

A special kernel code model '-mcmodel=kernel' is provided for system-level code, such as the Linux kernel. An important point to note is that by default on the AMD64 there is a 128-byte area of memory allocated below the stack pointer for temporary data, referred to as the "red-zone", which is not supported by the Linux kernel. Compilation of the Linux kernel on the AMD64 requires the options '-mcmodel=kernel -mno-red-zone'.

8.2 DEC Alpha options

The DEC Alpha processor has default settings which maximize floating-point performance, at the expense of full support for IEEE arithmetic features.

Support for infinity arithmetic and gradual underflow (denormalized numbers) is not enabled in the default configuration on the DEC Alpha processor. Operations which produce infinities or underflows will generate floating-point exceptions (also known as *traps*), and cause the program to terminate, unless the operating system catches and handles the exceptions (which is, in general, inefficient). The IEEE standard specifies that these operations should produce special results to represent the quantities in the IEEE numeric format.

In most cases the DEC Alpha default behavior is acceptable, since the majority of programs do not produce infinities or underflows. For applications which require these features, GCC provides the option '-mieee' to enable full support for IEEE arithmetic.

To demonstrate the difference between the two cases the following program divides 1 by 0:

```
#include <stdio.h>

int
main (void)
{
  double x = 1.0, y = 0.0;
  printf ("x/y = %g\n", x / y);
  return 0;
}
```

In IEEE arithmetic the result of 1/0 is inf (*Infinity*). If the program is compiled for the Alpha processor with the default settings it generates an exception, which terminates the program:

```
$ gcc -Wall alpha.c
$ ./a.out
```

Floating point exception   (on an Alpha processor)

Using the '-mieee' option ensures full IEEE compliance – the division 1/0 correctly produces the result inf and the program continues executing successfully:

```
$ gcc -Wall -mieee alpha.c
$ ./a.out
x/y = inf
```

Note that programs which generate floating-point exceptions run more slowly when compiled with '-mieee', because the exceptions are handled in software rather than hardware.

8.3 SPARC options

On the SPARC range of processors the '-mcpu=*CPU*' option generates processor-specific code. The valid options for *CPU* are v7, v8 (Super-SPARC), Sparclite, Sparclet and v9 (UltraSPARC). Code produced with a specific '-mcpu' option will not run on other processors in the SPARC family, except where supported by the backwards-compatibility of the processor itself.

On 64-bit UltraSPARC systems the options '-m32' and '-m64' control code generation for 32-bit or 64-bit environments. The 32-bit environment selected by '-m32' uses int, long and pointer types with a size of 32 bits. The 64-bit environment selected by '-m64' uses a 32-bit int type and 64-bit long and pointer types.

8.4 POWER/PowerPC options

On systems using the POWER/PowerPC family of processors the option '-mcpu=*CPU*' selects code generation for specific CPU models. The possible values of *CPU* include 'power', 'power2', 'powerpc', 'powerpc64' and 'common', in addition to other more specific model numbers. Code generated with the option '-mcpu=common' will run on any of the processors. The option '-maltivec' enables use of the Altivec vector processing instructions, if the appropriate hardware support is available.

The POWER/PowerPC processors include a combined "multiply and add" instruction $a * x + b$, which performs the two operations simultaneously for speed—this is referred to as a *fused* multiply and add, and is used by GCC by default. Due to differences in the way intermediate values are rounded, the result of a fused instruction may not be exactly the same as performing the two operations separately. In cases where strict IEEE arithmetic is required, the use of the combined instructions can be disabled with the option '-mno-fused-madd'.

On AIX systems, the option '-mminimal-toc' decreases the number of entries GCC puts in the global *table of contents* (TOC) in executables, to avoid "TOC overflow" errors at link time. The option '-mxl-call' makes the linking of object files from GCC compatible with those from IBM's XL compilers. For applications using POSIX threads, AIX always requires the option '-pthread' when compiling, even when the program will only run in single-threaded mode.

8.5 Multi-architecture support

A number of platforms can execute code for more than one architecture. For example, 64-bit platforms such as AMD64, MIPS64, Sparc64, and PowerPC64 support the execution of both 32-bit and 64-bit code. Similarly, ARM processors support both ARM code and a more compact code called "Thumb". GCC can be built to support multiple architectures on these platforms. By default, the compiler will generate 64-bit object files, but giving the '-m32' option will generate a 32-bit object file for the corresponding architecture.[5]

Note that support for multiple architectures depends on the corresponding libraries being available. On 64-bit platforms supporting both 64 and 32-bit executables, the 64-bit libraries are often placed in 'lib64' directories instead of 'lib' directories, e.g. in '/usr/lib64' and '/lib64'. The 32-bit libraries are then found in the default 'lib' directories as on other platforms. This allows both a 32-bit and a 64-bit library with the same name to exist on the same system. Other systems, such as the IA64/Itanium, use the directories '/usr/lib' and '/lib' for 64-bit libraries. GCC knows about these paths and uses the appropriate path when compiling 64-bit or 32-bit code.

8.6 Floating-point issues

The IEEE-754 standard defines the bit-level behavior of floating-point arithmetic operations on all modern processors. This allows numerical programs to be ported between different platforms with identical results, in principle. In practice, there are often minor variations caused by differences in the order of operations (depending on the compiler and optimization level) but these are generally not significant.

However, more noticeable discrepancies can be seen when porting numerical programs between x86 systems and other platforms, because the the x87 floating point unit (FPU) on x86 processors computes results using

---

[5] The options '-maix64' and '-maix32' are used on AIX.

extended precision internally (the values being converted to double precision only when they are stored to memory). In contrast, processors such as SPARC, PA-RISC, Alpha, MIPS and POWER/PowerPC work with native double-precision values throughout.[6] The differences between these implementations lead to changes in rounding and underflow/overflow behavior, because intermediate values have a greater relative precision and exponent range when computed in extended precision.[7] In particular, comparisons involving extended precision values may fail where the equivalent double precision values would compare equal.

To avoid these incompatibilities, the x87 FPU also offers a hardware double-precision rounding mode. In this mode the results of each extended-precision floating-point operation are rounded to double precision in the floating-point registers by the FPU. It is important to note that the rounding only affects the precision, not the exponent range, so the result is a hybrid double-precision format with an extended range of exponents.

On BSD systems such as FreeBSD, NetBSD and OpenBSD, the hardware double-precision rounding mode is the default, giving the greatest compatibility with native double precision platforms. On x86 GNU/Linux systems the default mode is extended precision (with the aim of providing increased accuracy). To enable the double-precision rounding mode it is necessary to override the default setting on per-process basis using the FLDCW "floating-point load control-word" machine instruction.[8] A simple function which can be called to execute this instruction is shown below. It uses the GCC extension keyword asm to insert the specified instruction in the assembly language output:

```
void
set_fpu (unsigned int mode)
{
    asm ("fldcw %0" : : "m" (*&mode));
}
```

The appropriate mode setting for double-precision rounding is 0x27F. The mode value also controls the floating-point exception handling behavior and rounding-direction (see the Intel and AMD processor reference manuals for details).

---

[6] Motorola 68k processors also use extended precision registers, like the x86.

[7] For quantities held in the x87 extended-precision registers the relative precision is 5.42×10^{-20} and the exponent range is $10^{\pm 4932}$. Standard double precision values have a relative precision of 2.22×10^{-16} and an exponent range of $10^{\pm 308}$.

[8] The operating system saves and restores the control word when switching between processes, so that each process maintains its own setting.

On x86 GNU/Linux, the function above can be called at the start of any program to disable excess precision. This will then reproduce the results of native double-precision processors, in the absence of underflows and overflows.

The following program demonstrates the different rounding modes:

```
#include <stdio.h>

void
set_fpu (unsigned int mode)
{
  asm ("fldcw %0" : : "m" (*&mode));
}

int
main (void)
{
  double a = 3.0, b = 7.0, c;
#ifdef DOUBLE
  set_fpu (0x27F);  /* use double-precision rounding */
#endif
  c = a / b;

  if (c == a / b) {
    printf ("comparison succeeds\n");
  } else {
    printf ("unexpected result\n");
  }
  return 0;
}
```

On x86 GNU/Linux systems the comparison c == a / b can produce an unexpected result if c is taken from memory (double precision) while a / b is computed in extended precision, because the fraction 3/7 has different representations in double and extended precision.

```
$ gcc -Wall fptest.c
$ ./a.out
unexpected result
```

Setting the hardware rounding mode to double precision prevents this from happening:

```
$ gcc -Wall -DDOUBLE fptest.c
$ ./a.out
comparison succeeds
```

Note that the floating-point control word affects the whole environment of the process, including any C Library functions that are called. One consequence of this is that long double arithmetic is effectively reduced to double precision, since it relies on extended precision operations.

The floating point control word only affects the behavior of the x87 FPU. Floating point operations computed with SSE and SSE2 instructions are always carried out in native double precision. Thus, the combined options

```
$ gcc -Wall -msse2 -mfpmath=sse  ...
```

are often sufficient to remove the effects of extended-precision. However, some operations (such as transcendental functions) are not available in the SSE/SSE2 extensions and will still be computed on the x87 FPU.

8.7 Portability of signed and unsigned types

The C and C++ standards allows the character type char to be signed or unsigned, depending on the platform and compiler. Most systems, including x86 GNU/Linux and Microsoft Windows, use signed char, but those based on PowerPC and ARM processors typically use unsigned char.[9] This can lead to unexpected results when porting programs between platforms which have different defaults for the type of char.

The following code demonstrates the difference between platforms with signed and unsigned char types:

```
#include <stdio.h>

int
main (void)
{
  char c = 255;
  if (c > 128) {
    printf("char is unsigned (c = %d)\n", c);
  } else {
    printf("char is signed (c = %d)\n", c);
  }
  return 0;
}
```

With an unsigned char, the variable c takes the value 255, but with a signed char it becomes −1.

---

[9] MacOS X (Darwin) on PowerPC uses signed char, for consistency with other Darwin architectures.

The correct way to manipulate char variables in C is through the portable functions declared in 'ctype.h', such as isalpha, isdigit and isblank, rather than by their numerical values. The behavior of non-portable conditional expressions such as c > 'a' depends on the signedness of the char type. If the signed or unsigned version of char is explicitly required at certain points in a program, it can be specified using the declarations signed char or unsigned char.

For existing programs which assume that char is signed or unsigned, GCC provides the options '-fsigned-char' and '-funsigned-char' to set the default type of char. Using these options, the example code above compiles cleanly when char is unsigned:

```
$ gcc -Wall -funsigned-char signed.c
$ ./a.out
char is unsigned (c = 255)
```

However, when char is signed the value 255 wraps around to -1, giving a warning:

```
$ gcc -Wall -fsigned-char signed.c
signed.c: In function 'main':
signed.c:7: warning: comparison is always false due to
   limited range of data type
$ ./a.out
char is signed (c = -1)
```

The warning message *"comparison is always true/false due to limited range of data type"* is one symptom of code which assumes a definition of char which is different from the actual type.

The most common problem with code written assuming signed char types occurs with the functions getc, fgetc and getchar (which read a character from a file). They have a return type of int, not char, and this allows them to use the special value -1 (defined as EOF) to indicate an end-of-file error. Unfortunately, many programs have been written which incorrectly store this return value straight into a char variable. Here is a typical example:

```
#include <stdio.h>

int
main (void)
{
   char c;
   while ((c = getchar()) != EOF) /* not portable */
      {
         printf ("read c = '%c'\n", c);
      }
```

```
    return 0;
}
```

This only works on platforms which default to a signed char type.[10] On platforms which use an unsigned char the same code will fail, because the value −1 becomes 255 when stored in an unsigned char. This usually causes an infinite loop because the end of the file cannot be recognized.[11] To be portable, the program should test the return value as an integer before coercing it to a char, as follows:

```
#include <stdio.h>

int
main (void)
{
  int i;
  while ((i = getchar()) != EOF)
    {
      unsigned char c = i;
      printf ("read c = '%c'\n", c);
    }
  return 0;
}
```

The same considerations described in this section apply to the definitions of bitfields in structs, which can be signed or unsigned by default. In GCC, the default type of bitfields can be controlled using the options '-fsigned-bitfields' and '-funsigned-bitfields'.

---

[10] There is also a subtle error even on platforms with signed char—the ASCII character 255 is spuriously interpreted as an end of file condition.

[11] If displayed, character code 255 often appears as ÿ.

9 Troubleshooting

GCC provides several help and diagnostic options to assist in trou-
bleshooting problems with the compilation process. All the options described in this chapter work with both gcc and g++.

9.1 Help for command-line options

To obtain a brief reminder of various command-line options, GCC provides
a help option which displays a summary of the top-level GCC command-
line options:

```
$ gcc --help
```

To display a complete list of options for gcc and its associated programs,
such as the GNU Linker and GNU Assembler, use the help option above
with the verbose ('-v') option:

```
$ gcc -v --help
```

The complete list of options produced by this command is extremely
long—you may wish to page through it using the more command, or
redirect the output to a file for reference:

```
$ gcc -v --help 2>&1 | more
```

9.2 Version numbers

You can find the version number of gcc using the version option:

```
$ gcc --version
gcc (GCC) 3.3.1
```

The version number is important when investigating compilation problems, since older versions of GCC may be missing some features that a program uses. The version number has the form *major-version.minor-version*
or *major-version.minor-version.micro-version*, where the additional third
"micro" version number (as shown above) is used for subsequent bug-fix
releases in a release series.

More details about the version can be found using '-v':

```
$ gcc -v
Reading specs from /usr/lib/gcc-lib/i686/3.3.1/specs
Configured with: ../configure --prefix=/usr
Thread model: posix
gcc version 3.3.1
```

This includes information on the build flags of the compiler itself and the
installed configuration file, 'specs'.

9.3 Verbose compilation

The '-v' option can also be used to display detailed information about the
exact sequence of commands used to compile and link a program. Here
is an example which shows the verbose compilation of the *Hello World*
program:

```
$ gcc -v -Wall hello.c
Reading specs from /usr/lib/gcc-lib/i686/3.3.1/specs
Configured with: ../configure --prefix=/usr
Thread model: posix
gcc version 3.3.1
 /usr/lib/gcc-lib/i686/3.3.1/cc1 -quiet -v -D__GNUC__=3
 -D__GNUC_MINOR__=3 -D__GNUC_PATCHLEVEL__=1
 hello.c -quiet -dumpbase hello.c -auxbase hello -Wall
 -version -o /tmp/cceCee26.s
GNU C version 3.3.1 (i686-pc-linux-gnu)
 compiled by GNU C version 3.3.1 (i686-pc-linux-gnu)
GGC heuristics: --param ggc-min-expand=51
 --param ggc-min-heapsize=40036
ignoring nonexistent directory "/usr/i686/include"
#include "..." search starts here:
#include <...> search starts here:
 /usr/local/include
 /usr/include
 /usr/lib/gcc-lib/i686/3.3.1/include
 /usr/include
End of search list.
 as -V -Qy -o /tmp/ccQynbTm.o /tmp/cceCee26.s
GNU assembler version 2.12.90.0.1 (i386-linux)
using BFD version 2.12.90.0.1 20020307 Debian/GNU
Linux
/usr/lib/gcc-lib/i686/3.3.1/collect2
 --eh-frame-hdr -m elf_i386 -dynamic-linker
 /lib/ld-linux.so.2 /usr/lib/crt1.o /usr/lib/crti.o
 /usr/lib/gcc-lib/i686/3.3.1/crtbegin.o
 -L/usr/lib/gcc-lib/i686/3.3.1
 -L/usr/lib/gcc-lib/i686/3.3.1/../../.. /tmp/ccQynbTm.o
 -lgcc -lgcc_eh -lc -lgcc -lgcc_eh
 /usr/lib/gcc-lib/i686/3.3.1/crtend.o
 /usr/lib/crtn.o
```

The output produced by '-v' can be useful whenever there is a problem
with the compilation process itself. It displays the full directory paths

used to search for header files and libraries, the predefined preprocessor symbols, and the object files and libraries used for linking.

9.4 Stopping a program in an infinite loop

A program which goes into an infinite loop or "hangs" can be difficult to debug. On most systems a foreground process can be stopped by hitting *Control-C*, which sends it an interrupt signal (SIGINT). However, this does not help in debugging the problem—the SIGINT signal terminates the process without producing a core dump. A more sophisticated approach is to *attach* to the running process with a debugger and inspect it interactively.

For example, here is a simple program with an infinite loop:

```
int
main (void)
{
  usigned int i = 0;
  while (1) { i++; };
  return 0;
}
```

In order to attach to the program and debug it, the code should be compiled with the debugging option '-g':

```
$ gcc -Wall -g loop.c
$ ./a.out
(program hangs)
```

Once the executable is running we need to find its process id (PID). This can be done from another session with the command ps x:

```
$ ps x
PID TTY    STAT TIME COMMAND
... .....  .    ....
891 pts/1  R    0:11 ./a.out
```

In this case the process id is 891, and we can now attach to it with gdb. The debugger should be started in the directory containing the executable and its source code:[1]

```
$ gdb a.out
(gdb) attach 891
Attaching to program: a.out, process 891
Reading symbols from /lib/libc.so.6...done.
Loaded symbols for /lib/libc.so.6
```

---

[1] Alternatively, the appropriate paths can be set up in gdb using the file and directory commands.

```
Reading symbols from /lib/ld-linux.so.2...done.
Loaded symbols for /lib/ld-linux.so.2
0x080483d4 in main () at loop.c:5
5            while (1) { i++; };
(gdb)
```

The output shows the line that was about to execute at the point when the
debugger attached to the process. The attached program is paused but
still "live"—it can be examined interactively and continued or terminated
(with the kill command) if necessary:

```
(gdb) print i
$1 = 1213315528
(gdb) kill
Kill the program being debugged? (y or n) y
(gdb)
```

If you want to stop a process immediately and create a core dump, the
shell command kill -3 *pid* (where *pid* is the process id) will send it
a SIGQUIT signal. The SIGQUIT signal does trigger a core dump, unlike
SIGINT. Note that if core dumps were disabled when the process was
started, no core file will be produced (see Section 5.1 [Examining core
files], page 41).

9.5 Preventing excessive memory usage

Sometimes a programming error will cause a process to allocate huge
amounts of memory, consuming all the RAM on a system. To prevent
this, the GNU Bash command ulimit -v *limit* can be used to restrict
the amount of virtual memory available to each process. The limit is
measured in kilobytes and applies to new processes started in the current
shell. For example,

```
$ ulimit -v 4096
```

will limit subsequent processes to 4 megabytes of virtual memory (4096k).
By default the limit cannot be increased in the same session once it has
been applied, so it is best to start a separate shell for reduced ulimit
operations. Alternatively, you can set a *soft limit* (which can be undone)
with the options '-S -v'.

In addition to preventing run-away processes, limiting the amount of
memory a program is allowed to allocate also provides a way to test how
robustly *out of memory* conditions are handled. An artificially low limit
can be used to simulate running out of memory—a well-written program
should not crash in this case.

The ulimit command supports other options including '-p', which
restricts the number of child processes that can be created, and '-t',

which places a limit on the number of CPU seconds that a process can run for. The complete list of settings can be shown with the command ulimit -a. To display more information about the ulimit command, type help ulimit at the Bash prompt.

10 Compiler-related tools

This chapter describes a number of tools which are useful in combination
with GCC. These include the GNU archiver ar, for creating libraries, and
the GNU profiling and coverage testing programs, gprof and gcov.

10.1 Creating a library with the GNU archiver

The GNU archiver ar combines a collection of object files into a single
archive file, also known as a *library*. An archive file is simply a convenient
way of distributing a large number of related object files together (as
described earlier in Section 2.7 [Linking with external libraries], page 15).

   To demonstrate the use of the GNU archiver we will create a small
library 'libhello.a' containing two functions hello and bye.

   The first object file will be generated from the source code for the
hello function, in the file 'hello_fn.c' seen earlier:

```
#include <stdio.h>
#include "hello.h"

void
hello (const char * name)
{
  printf ("Hello, %s!\n", name);
}
```

The second object file will be generated from the source file 'bye_fn.c',
which contains the new function bye:

```
#include <stdio.h>
#include "hello.h"

void
bye (void)
{
  printf ("Goodbye!\n");
}
```

Both functions use the header file 'hello.h', now with a prototype for
the function bye():

```
void hello (const char * name);
void bye (void);
```

The source code can be compiled to the object files 'hello_fn.o' and
'bye_fn.o' using the commands:

```
$ gcc -Wall -c hello_fn.c
$ gcc -Wall -c bye_fn.c
```

These object files can be combined into a static library using the following command line:

```
$ ar cr libhello.a hello_fn.o bye_fn.o
```

The option 'cr' stands for "create and replace".[1] If the library does not exist, it is first created. If the library already exists, any original files in it with the same names are replaced by the new files specified on the command line. The first argument 'libhello.a' is the name of the library. The remaining arguments are the names of the object files to be copied into the library.

The archiver ar also provides a "table of contents" option 't' to list the object files in an existing library:

```
$ ar t libhello.a
hello_fn.o
bye_fn.o
```

Note that when a library is distributed, the header files for the public functions and variables it provides should also be made available, so that the end-user can include them and obtain the correct prototypes.

We can now write a program using the functions in the newly created library:

```
#include "hello.h"

int
main (void)
{
  hello ("everyone");
  bye ();
  return 0;
}
```

This file can be compiled with the following command line, as described in Section 2.7 [Linking with external libraries], page 15, assuming the library 'libhello.a' is stored in the current directory:

```
$ gcc -Wall main.c libhello.a -o hello
```

The main program is linked against the object files found in the library file 'libhello.a' to produce the final executable.

The short-cut library linking option '-l' can also be used to link the program, without needing to specify the full filename of the library explicitly:

---

[1] Note that ar does not require a prefix '-' for its options.

```
$ gcc -Wall -L. main.c -lhello -o hello
```
The option '-L.' is needed to add the current directory to the library search path. The resulting executable can be run as usual:
```
$ ./hello
Hello, everyone!
Goodbye!
```
It displays the output from both the hello and bye functions defined in the library.

10.2 Using the profiler gprof

The GNU profiler gprof is a useful tool for measuring the performance of a program—it records the number of calls to each function and the amount of time spent there, on a per-function basis. Functions which consume a large fraction of the run-time can be identified easily from the output of gprof. Efforts to speed up a program should concentrate first on those functions which dominate the total run-time.

We will use gprof to examine the performance of a small numerical program which computes the lengths of sequences occurring in the unsolved *Collatz conjecture* in mathematics.[2] The Collatz conjecture involves sequences defined by the rule:

$$x_{n+1} \leftarrow \begin{cases} x_n/2 & \text{if } x_n \text{ is even} \\ 3x_n + 1 & \text{if } x_n \text{ is odd} \end{cases}$$

The sequence is iterated from an initial value x_0 until it terminates with the value 1. According to the conjecture, all sequences do terminate eventually—the program below displays the longest sequences as x_0 increases. The source file 'collatz.c' contains three functions: main, nseq and step:

```
#include <stdio.h>

/* Computes the length of Collatz sequences */

unsigned int
step (unsigned int x)
{
  if (x % 2 == 0)
    {
      return (x / 2);
    }
  else
    {
```

----

[2] American Mathematical Monthly, Volume 92 (1985), 3–23

```
      return (3 * x + 1);
    }
}

unsigned int
nseq (unsigned int x0)
{
  unsigned int i = 1, x;

  if (x0 == 1 || x0 == 0)
    return i;

  x = step (x0);

  while (x != 1 && x != 0)
    {
      x = step (x);
      i++;
    }

  return i;
}

int
main (void)
{
  unsigned int i, m = 0, im = 0;

  for (i = 1; i < 500000; i++)
    {
      unsigned int k = nseq (i);

      if (k > m)
        {
          m = k;
          im = i;
          printf ("sequence length = %u for %u\n", m, im);
        }
    }

  return 0;
}
```

To use profiling, the program must be compiled and linked with the '-pg' profiling option:

```
$ gcc -Wall -c -pg collatz.c
$ gcc -Wall -pg collatz.o
```

This creates an *instrumented* executable which contains additional instructions that record the time spent in each function.

If the program consists of more than one source file then the '-pg' option should be used when compiling each source file, and used again when linking the object files to create the final executable (as shown above). Forgetting to link with the option '-pg' is a common error, which prevents profiling from recording any useful information.

The executable must be run to create the profiling data:

```
$ ./a.out
```
(normal program output is displayed)

While running the instrumented executable, profiling data is silently written to a file 'gmon.out' in the current directory. It can be analyzed with gprof by giving the name of the executable as an argument:

```
$ gprof a.out
Flat profile:
Each sample counts as 0.01 seconds.
  %      cumul.    self               self    total
 time  seconds seconds    calls us/call us/call name
 68.59    2.14    2.14 62135400    0.03    0.03 step
 31.09    3.11    0.97   499999    1.94    6.22 nseq
  0.32    3.12    0.01                          main
```

The first column of the data shows that the program spends most of its time (almost 70%) in the function step, and 30% in nseq. Consequently efforts to decrease the run-time of the program should concentrate on the former. In comparison, the time spent within the main function itself is completely negligible (less than 1%).

The other columns in the output provide information on the total number of function calls made, and the time spent in each function. Additional output breaking down the run-time further is also produced by gprof but not shown here. Full details can be found in the manual "*GNU gprof—The GNU Profiler*", by Jay Fenlason and Richard Stallman.

10.3 Coverage testing with gcov

The GNU coverage testing tool gcov analyses the number of times each line of a program is executed during a run. This makes it possible to find areas of the code which are not used, or which are not exercised in testing. When combined with profiling information from gprof the information from coverage testing allows efforts to speed up a program to be concentrated on specific lines of the source code.

We will use the example program below to demonstrate gcov. This program loops overs the integers 1 to 9 and tests their divisibility with the modulus (%) operator.

```
#include <stdio.h>
```

```
int
main (void)
{
  int i;

  for (i = 1; i < 10; i++)
    {
      if (i % 3 == 0)
        printf ("%d is divisible by 3\n", i);
      if (i % 11 == 0)
        printf ("%d is divisible by 11\n", i);
    }

  return 0;
}
```

To enable coverage testing the program must be compiled with the following options:

```
$ gcc -Wall -fprofile-arcs -ftest-coverage cov.c
```

This creates an *instrumented* executable which contains additional instructions that record the number of times each line of the program is executed. The option '-ftest-coverage' adds instructions for counting the number of times individual lines are executed, while '-fprofile-arcs' incorporates instrumentation code for each branch of the program. Branch instrumentation records how frequently different paths are taken through 'if' statements and other conditionals. The executable must then be run to create the coverage data:

```
$ ./a.out
3 is divisible by 3
6 is divisible by 3
9 is divisible by 3
```

The data from the run is written to several files with the extensions '.bb' '.bbg' and '.da' respectively in the current directory. This data can be analyzed using the gcov command and the name of a source file:

```
$ gcov cov.c
 88.89% of 9 source lines executed in file cov.c
Creating cov.c.gcov
```

The gcov command produces an annotated version of the original source file, with the file extension '.gcov', containing counts of the number of times each line was executed:

```
        #include <stdio.h>
```

```
            int
            main (void)
            {
     1        int i;

    10        for (i = 1; i < 10; i++)
                {
     9            if (i % 3 == 0)
     3              printf ("%d is divisible by 3\n", i);
     9            if (i % 11 == 0)
######            printf ("%d is divisible by 11\n", i);
     9        }

     1        return 0;
     1    }
```

The line counts can be seen in the first column of the output. Lines which were not executed are marked with hashes '######'. The command 'grep '######' *.gcov' can be used to find parts of a program which have not been used.

11 How the compiler works

This chapter describes in more detail how GCC transforms source files to an executable file. Compilation is a multi-stage process involving several tools, including the GNU Compiler itself (through the gcc or g++ frontends), the GNU Assembler as, and the GNU Linker ld. The complete set of tools used in the compilation process is referred to as a *toolchain*.

11.1 An overview of the compilation process

The sequence of commands executed by a single invocation of GCC consists of the following stages:

- preprocessing (to expand macros)

- compilation (from source code to assembly language)

- assembly (from assembly language to machine code)

- linking (to create the final executable)

As an example, we will examine these compilation stages individually using the *Hello World* program 'hello.c':

```
#include <stdio.h>

int
main (void)
{
  printf ("Hello, world!\n");
  return 0;
}
```

Note that it is not necessary to use any of the individual commands described in this section to compile a program. All the commands are executed automatically and transparently by GCC internally, and can be seen using the '-v' option described earlier (see Section 9.3 [Verbose compilation], page 76). The purpose of this chapter is to provide an understanding of how the compiler works.

Although the *Hello World* program is very simple it uses external header files and libraries, and so exercises all the major steps of the compilation process.

11.2 The preprocessor

The first stage of the compilation process is the use of the preprocessor
to expand macros and included header files. To perform this stage, GCC
executes the following command:[1]

```
$ cpp hello.c > hello.i
```

The result is a file 'hello.i' which contains the source code with all
macros expanded. By convention, preprocessed files are given the file
extension '.i' for C programs and '.ii' for C++ programs. In practice,
the preprocessed file is not saved to disk unless the '-save-temps' option
is used.

11.3 The compiler

The next stage of the process is the actual compilation of preprocessed
source code to assembly language, for a specific processor. The command-
line option '-S' instructs gcc to convert the preprocessed C source code
to assembly language without creating an object file:

```
$ gcc -Wall -S hello.i
```

The resulting assembly language is stored in the file 'hello.s'. Here is
what the *Hello World* assembly language for an Intel x86 (i686) processor
looks like:

```
$ cat hello.s
      .file   "hello.c"
      .section  .rodata
.LC0:
      .string  "Hello, world!\n"
      .text
.globl main
      .type   main, @function
main:
      pushl  %ebp
      movl   %esp, %ebp
      subl   $8, %esp
      andl   $-16, %esp
      movl   $0, %eax
      subl   %eax, %esp
      movl   $.LC0, (%esp)
      call   printf
```

---

[1] As mentioned earlier, the preprocessor is integrated into the compiler in
recent versions of GCC. Conceptually, the compilation process is the same
as running the preprocessor as separate application.

```
movl   $0, %eax
leave
ret
.size  main, .-main
.ident "GCC: (GNU) 3.3.1"
```

Note that the assembly language contains a call to the external function
printf.

11.4 The assembler

The purpose of the assembler is to convert assembly language into machine code and generate an object file. When there are calls to external
functions in the assembly source file, the assembler leaves the addresses
of the external functions undefined, to be filled in later by the linker. The
assembler can be invoked with the following command line:

```
$ as hello.s -o hello.o
```

As with GCC, the output file is specified with the '-o' option. The resulting file 'hello.o' contains the machine instructions for the *Hello World*
program, with an undefined reference to printf.

11.5 The linker

The final stage of compilation is the linking of object files to create an
executable. In practice, an executable requires many external functions
from system and C run-time (crt) libraries. Consequently, the actual link
commands used internally by GCC are complicated. For example, the full
command for linking the *Hello World* program is:

```
$ ld -dynamic-linker /lib/ld-linux.so.2 /usr/lib/crt1.o
  /usr/lib/crti.o /usr/lib/gcc-lib/i686/3.3.1/crtbegin.o
  -L/usr/lib/gcc-lib/i686/3.3.1 hello.o -lgcc -lgcc_eh
  -lc -lgcc -lgcc_eh /usr/lib/gcc-lib/i686/3.3.1/crtend.o
  /usr/lib/crtn.o
```

Fortunately there is never any need to type the command above directly—
the entire linking process is handled transparently by gcc when invoked
as follows:

```
$ gcc hello.o
```

This links the object file 'hello.o' to the C standard library, and produces
an executable file 'a.out':

```
$ ./a.out
Hello, world!
```

An object file for a C++ program can be linked to the C++ standard library
in the same way with a single g++ command.

12 Examining compiled files

This chapter describes several useful tools for examining the contents of executable files and object files.

12.1 Identifying files

When a source file has been compiled to an object file or executable the options used to compile it are no longer obvious. The file command looks at the contents of an object file or executable and determines some of its characteristics, such as whether it was compiled with dynamic or static linking.

For example, here is the result of the file command for a typical executable:

```
$ file a.out
a.out: ELF 32-bit LSB executable, Intel 80386,
    version 1 (SYSV), dynamically linked (uses shared
    libs), not stripped
```

The output shows that the executable file is dynamically linked, and compiled for the Intel 386 and compatible processors. A full explanation of the output is shown below:

ELF   The internal format of the executable file (ELF stands for "Executable and Linking Format", other formats such as COFF "Common Object File Format" are used on some older operating systems (e.g. MS-DOS)).

32-bit
      The word size (for some platforms this would be 64-bit).

LSB   Compiled for a platform with *least significant byte* first word-ordering, such as Intel and AMD x86 processors (the alternative MSB *most significant byte* first is used by other processors, such as the Motorola 680x0)[1]. Some processors such as Itanium and MIPS support both LSB and MSB orderings.

Intel 80386
      The processor the executable file was compiled for.

version 1 (SYSV)
      This is the version of the internal format of the file.

---

[1]   The MSB and LSB orderings are also known as big-endian and little-endian respectively (the terms originate from Jonathan Swift's satire "Gulliver's Travels", 1727).

`dynamically linked`
> The executable uses shared libraries (`statically linked` indicates
> programs linked statically, for example using the '`-static`' option)

`not stripped`
> The executable contains a symbol table (this can be removed with
> the `strip` command).

The `file` command can also be used on object files, where it gives similar output. The POSIX standard[2] for Unix systems defines the behavior of the `file` command.

12.2 Examining the symbol table

As described earlier in the discussion of debugging, executables and object files can contain a symbol table (see Chapter 5 [Compiling for debugging], page 41). This table stores the location of functions and variables by name, and can be displayed with the nm command:

```
$ nm a.out
08048334 t Letext
08049498 ? _DYNAMIC
08049570 ? _GLOBAL_OFFSET_TABLE_
........
080483f0 T main
08049590 b object.11
0804948c d p.3
         U printf@GLIBC_2.0
```

Among the contents of the symbol table, the output shows that the start of the main function has the hexadecimal offset 080483f0. Most of the symbols are for internal use by the compiler and operating system. A 'T' in the second column indicates a function that is defined in the object file, while a 'U' indicates a function which is undefined (and should be resolved by linking against another object file). A complete explanation of the output of nm can be found in the *GNU Binutils* manual.

The most common use of the nm command is to check whether a library contains the definition of a specific function, by looking for a 'T' entry in the second column against the function name.

12.3 Finding dynamically linked libraries

When a program has been compiled using shared libraries it needs to load those libraries dynamically at run-time in order to call external functions.

---

[2] POSIX.1 (2003 edition), IEEE Std 1003.1-2003.

The command `ldd` examines an executable and displays a list of the shared libraries that it needs. These libraries are referred to as the shared library *dependencies* of the executable.

For example, the following commands demonstrate how to find the shared library dependencies of the *Hello World* program:

```
$ gcc -Wall hello.c
$ ldd a.out
libc.so.6 => /lib/libc.so.6 (0x40020000)
/lib/ld-linux.so.2 => /lib/ld-linux.so.2 (0x40000000)
```

The output shows that the *Hello World* program depends on the C library `libc` (shared library version 6) and the dynamic loader library `ld-linux` (shared library version 2).

If the program uses external libraries, such as the math library, these are also displayed. For example, the `calc` program (which uses the `sqrt` function) generates the following output:

```
$ gcc -Wall calc.c -lm -o calc
$ ldd calc
libm.so.6 => /lib/libm.so.6 (0x40020000)
libc.so.6 => /lib/libc.so.6 (0x40041000)
/lib/ld-linux.so.2 => /lib/ld-linux.so.2 (0x40000000)
```

The first line shows that this program depends on the math library `libm` (shared library version 6), in addition to the C library and dynamic loader library.

The `ldd` command can also be used to examine shared libraries themselves, in order to follow a chain of shared library dependencies.

13 Common error messages

This chapter describes the most frequent error and warning messages produced by gcc and g++. Each case is accompanied by a description of the causes, an example and suggestions of possible solutions.

13.1 Preprocessor error messages

No such file or directory

This error occurs if GCC cannot find a requested file on its search path. The file may have been specified on the command-line, or with a preprocessor #include statement. Either the filename has been spelled incorrectly or the directory for the file needs to be added to the include path or link path.

Example:

```
#include <stdoi.h>  /* incorrect */

int
main (void)
{
  printf ("Hello World!\n");
  return 0;
}
```

The program above tries to include the non-existent file 'stdoi.h' giving the error 'stdoi.h: No such file or directory'. The correct filename should be 'stdio.h'.

macro or '#include' recursion too deep
#include nested too deeply

This error occurs if the preprocessor encounters too many nested '#include' directives. It is usually caused by two or more files trying to include each other, leading to an infinite recursion.

Example:

```
/* foo.h */
#include "bar.h"
...
/* bar.h */
#include "foo.h"
...
```

The solution to this problem is to ensure that files do not mutually include each other, or to use "include guards" (see Section 7.4.2 [Providing your own templates], page 61 for an example).

`invalid preprocessing directive #...`

> This error indicates that the preprocessor encountered an unrecognized # command.

Example:

```
#if FOO
    int x = 1;
#elsif BAR    /* should be #elif */
    int x = 2;
#else
    int x = 3;
#endif
```

The preprocessor syntax requires #elif for the "else if" condition in #if blocks, rather than #elseif. In the example above an invalid directive error occurs at the incorrect usage #elseif, but only when FOO is defined (otherwise the preprocessor ignores everything up to the #else statement).

`warning: This file includes at least one deprecated or antiquated header.`

> This warning is generated for C++ programs which include old-style library header files, such as 'iostream.h', instead of the modern C++ library headers without the '.h' extension. The old headers import their functions into the top-level global namespace, instead of using the std:: namespace. Note that old-style header files are still supported, so this message is only a warning and existing programs will continue to compile. The message is actually generated by a #warning directive in the old header files, and not by the preprocessor itself.

Example:

```
#include <iostream.h>  /* old style */

int
main (void)
{
  cout << "Hello World!\n";
  return 0;
}
```

This program uses an old-style header file 'iostream.h'. It could be updated to use #include <iostream> and std::cout instead.

13.2 Compiler error messages

`'variable'` undeclared (first use in this function)

In C and C++ variables must be declared before they can be used. This error message indicates that the compiler has encountered a variable name which does not have a corresponding declaration. It can be caused by a missing declaration, or a typing error in the name. Variable names are case-sensitive, so `foo` and `Foo` represent different variables. To keep the output short, only the first use of an undeclared variable is reported.

Example:

```
int
main (void)
{
  int i;
  j = 0;      /* undeclared */
  return j;
}
```

The variable `j` is not declared and will trigger the error `'j'` undeclared.

parse error before `'...'`

syntax error

These error messages occur when the compiler encounters unexpected input, i.e. sequences of characters which do not follow the syntax of the language. The error messages can be triggered by a missing close bracket, brace or semicolon preceding the line of the error, or an invalid keyword.

Example:

```
#include <stdio.h>

int
main (void)
{
  printf ("Hello ")      /* missing semicolon */
  printf ("World!\n");
  return 0;
}
```

There is a missing semicolon after the first call to `printf`, giving a parse error.

parse error at end of input

This error occurs if the compiler encounters the end of a file unexpectedly, such as when it has parsed an unbalanced number of

opening and closing braces. It is often caused by a missing closing
brace somewhere.

Example:

```
#include <stdio.h>

int
main (void)
{
  if (1) {
    printf ("Hello World!\n");
    return 0;  /* no closing brace */
}
```

An additional closing brace is needed in this program to prevent
the error parse error at end of input.

`warning: implicit declaration of function '...'`

This warning is generated when a function is used without a prototype being declared. It can be caused by failing to include a header
file, or otherwise forgetting to provide a function prototype.

Example:

```
int
main (void)
{
  printf ("Hello World!\n");  /* no header */
  return 0;
}
```

The system header file 'stdio.h' is not included, so the prototype for printf is not declared. The program needs an initial line
#include <stdio.h>.

`unterminated string or character constant`

This error is caused by an opening string or character quote which
does not have a corresponding closing quote. Quotes must occur
in matching pairs, either single quotes 'a' for characters or double
quotes "aaa" for strings.

Example:

```
#include <stdio.h>

int
main (void)
{
  printf("Hello World!\n);  /* no closing quote */
  return 0;
```

```
        }
```

The opening quote for the string in this program does not have a corresponding closing quote, so the compiler will read the rest of the file as part of the string.

`character constant too long`

In C and C++ character codes are written using single quotes, e.g. `'a'` gives the ASCII code for the letter a (67), and `'\n'` gives the ASCII code for newline (10). This error occurs if single quotes are used to enclose more than one character.

Example:

```
#include <stdio.h>

int
main (void)
{
  printf ('Hello World!\n');   /* wrong quotes */
  return 0;
}
```

The program above confuses single-quotes and double-quotes. A sequence of characters should be written with double quotes, e.g. `"Hello World!"`. This same problem occurs in the following C++ program,

```
#include <iostream>

int
main (void)
{
  std::cout << 'Hello World!\n';   // wrong quotes
  return 0;
}
```

This error can also occur if the forward slash and backslash are confused in an escape sequence, e.g. using `'/n'` instead of `'\n'`. The sequence `/n` consists of two separate characters, `'/'` and `'n'`.

Note that according to the C standard there is no limit on the length of a character constant, but the value of a character constant that contains more than one character is implementation-defined. Recent versions of GCC provide support multi-byte character constants, and instead of an error the warnings `multiple-character character constant` or `warning: character constant too long for its type` are generated in this case.

`warning: initialization makes integer from pointer without a`
`cast`

> This error indicates a misuse of a pointer in an integer context. Technically, it is possible to convert between integer and pointer types, but this is rarely needed outside system-level applications. More often, this warning is the result of using a pointer without dereferencing it (e.g. writing int i = p instead of int i = *p).
>
> This warning can also occur with char and char * types, since char is an integer type.
>
> Example:

```
int
main (void)
{
    char c = "\n";  /* incorrect */
    return 0;
}
```

> The variable c has type char, while the string "\n" evaluates to a const char * pointer (to a 2-byte region of memory containing the ASCII value for newline followed by a zero byte '\0', since strings are null-terminated). The ASCII code for newline can be found using char c = '\n';
>
> Similar errors can occur with misuse of the macro NULL,

```
#include <stdlib.h>

int
main (void)
{
    int i = NULL;  /* incorrect */
    return 0;
}
```

> In C, the macro NULL is defined as ((void *)0) in 'stdlib.h' and should only be used in a pointer context.

`dereferencing pointer to incomplete type`

> This error occurs when a program attempts to access the elements of struct through a pointer without the layout of the struct being declared first. In C and C++ it is possible to declare pointers to structs before declaring their struct layout, provided the pointers are not dereferenced—this is known as *forward declaration*.
>
> Example:

```
struct btree * data;
```

```
    int
    main (void)
    {
      data->size = 0;   /* incomplete type */
      return 0;
    }
```

This program has a forward declaration of the btree struct data. However, the definition of the struct is needed before the pointer can be dereferenced to access individual members.

warning: unknown escape sequence '...'

This error is caused by an incorrect use of the escape character in a string. Valid escape sequences are:

\n newline	\t tab
\b backspace	\r carriage return
\f form feed	\v vertical tab
\a alert (bell)	

The combinations \\, \', \" and \? can be used for individual characters. Escape sequences can also use octal codes \0–\377 and hexadecimal codes \0x00–\0xFF.

Example:

```
    #include <stdio.h>

    int
    main (void)
    {
      printf ("HELLO WORLD!\N");
      return 0;
    }
```

The escape sequence \N in the program above is invalid—the correct escape sequence for a newline is \n.

warning: suggest parentheses around assignment used as truth value

This warning highlights a potentially serious error, using the assignment operator '=' instead of the comparison operator '==' in the test of a conditional statement or other logical expression. While the assignment operator can be used as part of a logical value, this is rarely the intended behavior.

Example:

```
    #include <stdio.h>

    int
```

```
main (void)
{
  int i = 0;
  if (i = 1) {  /* = should be == */
    printf ("unexpected result\n");
  }
  return 0;
}
```

The test above should be written as if (i == 1), otherwise the variable i will be set to 1 by the evaluation of the if statement itself. The operator '=' both assigns and returns the value of its right-hand side, causing the variable i to be modified and the unexpected branch taken. Similar unexpected results occur with if (i = 0) instead of if (i == 0), except that in this case the body of the if statement would never be executed.

This warning is suppressed if the assignment is enclosed in additional parentheses to indicate that it is being used legitimately.

warning: control reaches end of non-void function

A function which has been declared with a return type, such as int or double, should always have a return statement returning a value of the corresponding type at all possible end points—otherwise its return value is not well-defined. Functions declared void do not need return statements.

Example:

```
#include <stdio.h>

int
display (const char * str)
{
  printf ("%s\n", str);
}
```

The program above reaches the end of the display function, which has a return type of int, without a return statement. An additional line such as return 0; is needed.

When using gcc the main function of a C program must return a value of type int (the exit status of the program). In C++ the return statement can be omitted from the main function—the return value of the C++ main function defaults to 0 if unspecified.

warning: unused variable '...'
warning: unused parameter '...'

These warnings indicate that a variable has been declared as a local variable or in the parameters of a function, but has not been used anywhere. An unused variable can be the result of a programming error, such as accidentally using the name of a different variable in place of the intended one.

Example:

```
int
foo (int k, char * p)
{
    int i, j;
    j = k;
    return j;
}
```

In this program the variable i and the parameter p are never used. Note that unused variables are reported by '-Wall', while unused parameters are only shown with '-Wall -W'.

`warning: passing arg of ... as ... due to prototype`

This warning occurs when a function is called with an argument of a different type from that specified in the prototype. The option '-Wconversion' is needed to enable this warning. See the description of '-Wconversion' in Section 3.5 [Additional warning options], page 31 for an example.

`warning: assignment of read-only location`
`warning: cast discards qualifiers from pointer target type`
`warning: assignment discards qualifiers ...`
`warning: initialization discards qualifiers ...`
`warning: return discards qualifiers ...`

These warnings occur when a pointer is used incorrectly, violating a type qualifier such as const. Data accessed through a pointer marked as const should not be modified, and the pointer itself can only be assigned to other pointers that are also marked const.

Example:

```
char *
f (const char *s)
{
    *s = '\0';  /* assigns to read-only data */
    return s;   /* discards const */
}
```

This program attempts to modify constant data, and to discard the const property of the argument s in the return value.

`initializer element is not a constant`

In C, global variables can only be initialized with constants, such as numeric values, NULL or fixed strings. This error occurs if a non-constant value is used.

Example:

```
#include <stdio.h>

FILE *stream = stdout;   /* not constant */
int i = 10;
int j = 2 * i;           /* not constant */

int
main (void)
{
  fprintf (stream, "Hello World!\n");
  return 0;
}
```

This program attempts to initialize two variables from other variables. In particular, the stream stdout is not required to be a constant by the C standard (although on some systems it is a constant). Note that non-constant initializers are allowed in C++.

13.3 Linker error messages

`file not recognized: File format not recognized`

GCC uses the extension of a file, such as '.c' or '.cc', to determine its content. If the extension is missing GCC cannot recognize the file type and will give this error.

Example:

```
#include <stdio.h>

int
main (void)
{
  printf ("Hello World!\n");
  return 0;
}
```

If the program above is saved in a file 'hello' without any extension then compiling it will give the error:

```
$ gcc -Wall hello
hello: file not recognized: File format not
recognized
```

```
collect2: ld returned 1 exit status
```

The solution is to rename the file to the correct extension, in this case 'hello.c'.

`undefined reference to 'foo'`
`collect2: ld returned 1 exit status`

This error occurs when a program uses a function or variable which is not defined in any of the object files or libraries supplied to the linker. It can be caused by a missing library or the use of an incorrect name. In the error message above, the program 'collect2' is part of the linker.

Example:

```
int foo(void);

int
main (void)
{
   foo();
   return 0;
}
```

If this program is compiled without linking to a library or object file containing the function foo() there will be an undefined reference error.

`/usr/lib/crt1.o(.text+0x18): undefined reference to 'main'`

This error is a special case of the error above, when the missing function is main. In C and C++, every program must have a main function (where execution starts). When compiling an individual source file without a main function, use the option '-c' (see Section 2.4.1 [Creating object files from source files], page 11).

13.4 Runtime error messages

`error while loading shared libraries:`
`cannot open shared object file: No such file or directory`

The program uses shared libraries, but the necessary shared library files cannot be found by the dynamic linker when the program starts. The search path for shared libraries is controlled by the environment variable LD_LIBRARY_PATH (see Section 3.2 [Shared libraries and static libraries], page 23).

`Segmentation fault`
`Bus error`

These runtime messages indicate a memory access error.

Common causes include:

- dereferencing a null pointer or uninitialized pointer
- out-of-bounds array access
- incorrect use of `malloc`, `free` and related functions
- use of `scanf` with invalid arguments

There is a subtle difference between segmentation faults and bus errors. A segmentation fault occurs when a process tries to access memory protected by the operating system. A bus error occurs when valid memory is accessed in an incorrect way (for example, trying to read an *unaligned* value on architectures where values must be aligned with 4-byte offsets).

floating point exception

This runtime error is caused by an arithmetic exception, such as division by zero, overflow, underflow or an invalid operation (e.g. taking the square root of -1). The operating system determines which conditions produce this error. On GNU systems, the functions `feenableexcept` and `fedisableexcept` can be used to trap or mask each type of exception.

Illegal instruction

This error is produced by the operating system when an illegal machine instruction is encountered. It occurs when code has been compiled for one specific architecture and run on another.

14 Getting help

If you encounter a problem not covered by this introduction, there are several reference manuals which describe GCC and language-related topics in more detail (see [Further reading], page 111). These manuals contain answers to common questions, and careful study of them will usually yield a solution.

Alternatively, there are many companies and consultants who offer commercial support for programming matters related to GCC on an hourly or ongoing basis. For businesses this can be a cost-effective way to obtain high-quality support.

A directory of free software support companies and their current rates can be found on the GNU Project website.[1] With free software, commercial support is available in a free market—service companies compete in quality and price, and users are not tied to any particular one. In contrast, support for proprietary software is usually only available from the original vendor.

A higher-level of commercial support for GCC is available from companies involved in the development of the GNU compiler toolchain itself. A listing of these companies can be found in the "Development Companies" section of the publisher's webpage for this book.[2] These companies can provide services such as extending GCC to generate code for new CPUs or fixing bugs in the compiler.

---

[1] http://www.gnu.org/prep/service.html

[2] http://www.network-theory.co.uk/gcc/intro/

Further reading

The definitive guide to GCC is the official reference manual, *"Using GCC"*, published by GNU Press:

> *Using GCC (for GCC version 3.3.1)* by Richard M. Stallman and the GCC Developer Community (Published by GNU Press, ISBN 1-882114-39-6)

This manual is essential for anyone working with GCC because it describes every option in detail. Note that the manual is updated when new releases of GCC become available, so the ISBN number may change in the future.

If you are new to programming with GCC you will also want to learn how to use the GNU Debugger GDB, and how to compile large programs easily with GNU Make. These tools are described in the following manuals:

> *Debugging with GDB: The GNU Source-Level Debugger* by Richard M. Stallman, Roland Pesch, Stan Shebs, et al. (Published by GNU Press, ISBN 1-882114-88-4)

> *GNU Make: A Program for Directing Recompilation* by Richard M. Stallman and Roland McGrath (Published by GNU Press, ISBN 1-882114-82-5)

For effective C programming it is also essential to have a good knowledge of the C standard library. The following manual documents all the functions in the GNU C Library:

> *The GNU C Library Reference Manual* by Sandra Loosemore with Richard M. Stallman, et al (2 vols) (Published by GNU Press, ISBN 1-882114-22-1 and 1-882114-24-8)

Be sure to check the website `http://www.gnupress.org/` for the latest printed editions of manuals published by GNU Press. The manuals can be purchased online using a credit card at the FSF website[1] in addition to being available for order through most bookstores using the ISBNs. Manuals published by GNU Press raise funds for the Free Software Foundation and the GNU Project.

Information about shell commands, environment variables and shell-quoting rules can be found in the following book:

> *The GNU Bash Reference Manual* by Chet Ramey and Brian Fox (Published by Network Theory Ltd, ISBN 0-9541617-7-7)

Other GNU Manuals mentioned in this book (such as *GNU gprof—The GNU Profiler* and *The GNU Binutils Manual*) were not available in print

---

[1] `http://order.fsf.org/`

at the time this book went to press. Links to online copies can be found at the publisher's webpage for this book.[2]

The official GNU Project webpage for GCC can be found on the GNU website at http://www.gnu.org/software/gcc/. This includes a list of frequently asked questions, as well as the GCC bug tracking database and a lot of other useful information about GCC.

There are many books about the C and C++ languages themselves. Two of the standard references are:

> The C Programming Language (ANSI edition) Brian W. Kernighan, Dennis Ritchie (ISBN 0-13110362-8)

> The C++ Programming Language (3rd edition) Bjarne Strous-trup (ISBN 0-20188954-4)

Anyone using the C and C++ languages in a professional context should obtain a copy of the official language standards, which are also available as printed books:

> The C Standard: Incorporating Technical Corrigendum 1 (Pub-lished by Wiley, ISBN 0-470-84573-2)

> The C++ Standard (Published by Wiley, ISBN 0-470-84674-7)

For reference, the C standard number is ISO/IEC 9899:1990, for the orig-inal C standard published in 1990 and implemented by GCC. A revised C standard ISO/IEC 9899:1999 (known as C99) was published in 1999, and this is mostly (but not yet fully) supported by GCC. The C++ standard is ISO/IEC 14882.

The floating-point arithmetic standard IEEE-754 is important for any programs involving numerical computations. The standard is available commercially from the IEEE, and is also described in the following book:

> Numerical Computing with IEEE Floating Point Arithmetic by Michael Overton (Published by SIAM, ISBN 0-89871-482-6).

The book includes many examples to illustrate the rationale for the stan-dard.

---

[2] http://www.network-theory.co.uk/gcc/intro/

Acknowledgements

Many people have contributed to this book, and it is important to record their names here:

Thanks to Gerald Pfeifer, for his careful reviewing and numerous suggestions for improving the book.

Thanks to Andreas Jaeger, for information on AMD64 and multi-architecture support, and many helpful comments.

Thanks to David Edelsohn, for information on the POWER/PowerPC series of processors.

Thanks to Jamie Lokier, for research.

Thanks to Martin Leisner, Mario Pernici, Stephen Compall and Nigel Lowry, for helpful corrections.

Thanks to Gerard Jungman, for useful comments.

Thanks to Steven Rubin, for generating the chip layout for the cover with Electric.

And most importantly, thanks to Richard Stallman, founder of the GNU Project, for writing GCC and making it free software.

Other books from the publisher

Network Theory publishes books about free software under free documentation licenses. Our current catalogue includes the following titles:

- *Comparing and Merging Files with GNU diff and patch* by David MacKenzie, Paul Eggert, and Richard Stallman (ISBN 0-9541617-5-0) $19.95 (£12.95)

- *Version Management with CVS* by Per Cederqvist et al. (ISBN 0-9541617-1-8) $29.95 (£19.95)

- *GNU Bash Reference Manual* by Chet Ramey and Brian Fox (ISBN 0-9541617-7-7) $29.95 (£19.95)

- *An Introduction to R* by W.N. Venables, D.M. Smith and the R Development Core Team (ISBN 0-9541617-4-2) $19.95 (£12.95)

- *GNU Octave Manual* by John W. Eaton (ISBN 0-9541617-2-6) $29.99 (£19.99)

- *GNU Scientific Library Reference Manual—Second Edition* by M. Galassi, J. Davies, J. Theiler, B. Gough, G. Jungman, M. Booth, F. Rossi (ISBN 0-9541617-3-4) $39.99 (£24.99)

- *An Introduction to Python* by Guido van Rossum and Fred L. Drake, Jr. (ISBN 0-9541617-6-9) $19.95 (£12.95)

- *Python Language Reference Manual* by Guido van Rossum and Fred L. Drake, Jr. (ISBN 0-9541617-8-5) $19.95 (£12.95)

- *The R Reference Manual—Base Package (Volume 1)* by the R Development Core Team (ISBN 0-9546120-0-0) $69.95 (£39.95)

- *The R Reference Manual—Base Package (Volume 2)* by the R Development Core Team (ISBN 0-9546120-1-9) $69.95 (£39.95)

All titles are available for order from bookstores worldwide.

Sales of the manuals fund the development of more free software and documentation.

For details, visit the website http://www.network-theory.co.uk/

Free software organizations

The GNU Compiler Collection is part of the GNU Project, launched in 1984 to develop a complete Unix-like operating system which is free software: the GNU system.

The Free Software Foundation (FSF) is a tax-exempt charity that raises funds for continuing work on the GNU Project. It is dedicated to promoting the right to use, study, copy, modify, and redistribute computer programs. One of the best ways to help the development of free software is to become an associate member of the Free Software Foundation, and pay regular dues to support their efforts.

Associate members of the Free Software Foundation receive many benefits, including regular newsletters, admission to the FSF annual meeting, and discounts on books and CDROMs published by GNU Press. Membership dues are also tax deductible in the USA. For more information on becoming a member, visit the FSF website at `http://www.fsf.org/`.

The Free Software Foundation Europe (FSFE) is a sister organisation of the Free Software Foundation. The FSFE is active in promoting free software at all levels in Europe. For an annual membership fee, individuals can join FSFE and support its work. Members receive a personalised GPG-compatible membership smartcard, allowing secure digital authentication of email and files, and gain access to the "FSFE Fellowship", an electronic community for software freedom. For more information, visit the FSFE website at `http://www.fsfe.org/`.

The *Foundation for a Free Information Infrastructure (FFII)* is another important organization in Europe. FFII is not specific to free software, but works to defend the rights of all programmers and computer users against monopolies in the field of computing, such as patents on software. For more information about FFII, or to support their work with a donation, visit their website at `http://www.ffii.org/`.

GNU Free Documentation License

Version 1.2, November 2002

Copyright © 2000,2001,2002 Free Software Foundation, Inc.
51 Franklin St, Fifth Floor, Boston, MA 02110-1301, USA

Everyone is permitted to copy and distribute verbatim copies
of this license document, but changing it is not allowed.

0. PREAMBLE

The purpose of this License is to make a manual, textbook, or other functional
and useful document *free* in the sense of freedom: to assure everyone the effective freedom to copy and redistribute it, with or without modifying it, either
commercially or noncommercially. Secondarily, this License preserves for the author and publisher a way to get credit for their work, while not being considered
responsible for modifications made by others.

This License is a kind of "copyleft", which means that derivative works of the
document must themselves be free in the same sense. It complements the GNU
General Public License, which is a copyleft license designed for free software.

We have designed this License in order to use it for manuals for free software,
because free software needs free documentation: a free program should come with
manuals providing the same freedoms that the software does. But this License is
not limited to software manuals; it can be used for any textual work, regardless
of subject matter or whether it is published as a printed book. We recommend
this License principally for works whose purpose is instruction or reference.

1. APPLICABILITY AND DEFINITIONS

This License applies to any manual or other work, in any medium, that contains
a notice placed by the copyright holder saying it can be distributed under the
terms of this License. Such a notice grants a world-wide, royalty-free license,
unlimited in duration, to use that work under the conditions stated herein. The
"Document", below, refers to any such manual or work. Any member of the
public is a licensee, and is addressed as "you". You accept the license if you copy,
modify or distribute the work in a way requiring permission under copyright law.

A "Modified Version" of the Document means any work containing the Document
or a portion of it, either copied verbatim, or with modifications and/or translated
into another language.

A "Secondary Section" is a named appendix or a front-matter section of the
Document that deals exclusively with the relationship of the publishers or authors
of the Document to the Document's overall subject (or to related matters) and
contains nothing that could fall directly within that overall subject. (Thus, if
the Document is in part a textbook of mathematics, a Secondary Section may
not explain any mathematics.) The relationship could be a matter of historical
connection with the subject or with related matters, or of legal, commercial,
philosophical, ethical or political position regarding them.

The "Invariant Sections" are certain Secondary Sections whose titles are designated, as being those of Invariant Sections, in the notice that says that the
Document is released under this License. If a section does not fit the above definition of Secondary then it is not allowed to be designated as Invariant. The
Document may contain zero Invariant Sections. If the Document does not identify any Invariant Sections then there are none.

The "Cover Texts" are certain short passages of text that are listed, as Front-
Cover Texts or Back-Cover Texts, in the notice that says that the Document is

released under this License. A Front-Cover Text may be at most 5 words, and a Back-Cover Text may be at most 25 words.

A "Transparent" copy of the Document means a machine-readable copy, represented in a format whose specification is available to the general public, that is suitable for revising the document straightforwardly with generic text editors or (for images composed of pixels) generic paint programs or (for drawings) some widely available drawing editor, and that is suitable for input to text formatters or for automatic translation to a variety of formats suitable for input to text formatters. A copy made in an otherwise Transparent file format whose markup, or absence of markup, has been arranged to thwart or discourage subsequent modification by readers is not Transparent. An image format is not Transparent if used for any substantial amount of text. A copy that is not "Transparent" is called "Opaque".

Examples of suitable formats for Transparent copies include plain ASCII without markup, Texinfo input format, LaTeX input format, SGML or XML using a publicly available DTD, and standard-conforming simple HTML, PostScript or PDF designed for human modification. Examples of transparent image formats include PNG, XCF and JPG. Opaque formats include proprietary formats that can be read and edited only by proprietary word processors, SGML or XML for which the DTD and/or processing tools are not generally available, and the machine-generated HTML, PostScript or PDF produced by some word processors for output purposes only.

The "Title Page" means, for a printed book, the title page itself, plus such following pages as are needed to hold, legibly, the material this License requires to appear in the title page. For works in formats which do not have any title page as such, "Title Page" means the text near the most prominent appearance of the work's title, preceding the beginning of the body of the text.

A section "Entitled XYZ" means a named subunit of the Document whose title either is precisely XYZ or contains XYZ in parentheses following text that translates XYZ in another language. (Here XYZ stands for a specific section name mentioned below, such as "Acknowledgements", "Dedications", "Endorsements", or "History".) To "Preserve the Title" of such a section when you modify the Document means that it remains a section "Entitled XYZ" according to this definition.

The Document may include Warranty Disclaimers next to the notice which states that this License applies to the Document. These Warranty Disclaimers are considered to be included by reference in this License, but only as regards disclaiming warranties: any other implication that these Warranty Disclaimers may have is void and has no effect on the meaning of this License.

2. VERBATIM COPYING

You may copy and distribute the Document in any medium, either commercially or noncommercially, provided that this License, the copyright notices, and the license notice saying this License applies to the Document are reproduced in all copies, and that you add no other conditions whatsoever to those of this License. You may not use technical measures to obstruct or control the reading or further copying of the copies you make or distribute. However, you may accept compensation in exchange for copies. If you distribute a large enough number of copies you must also follow the conditions in section 3.

You may also lend copies, under the same conditions stated above, and you may publicly display copies.

3. COPYING IN QUANTITY

If you publish printed copies (or copies in media that commonly have printed covers) of the Document, numbering more than 100, and the Document's license notice requires Cover Texts, you must enclose the copies in covers that carry, clearly and legibly, all these Cover Texts: Front-Cover Texts on the front cover, and Back-Cover Texts on the back cover. Both covers must also clearly and legibly identify you as the publisher of these copies. The front cover must present the full title with all words of the title equally prominent and visible. You may add other material on the covers in addition. Copying with changes limited to the covers, as long as they preserve the title of the Document and satisfy these conditions, can be treated as verbatim copying in other respects.

If the required texts for either cover are too voluminous to fit legibly, you should put the first ones listed (as many as fit reasonably) on the actual cover, and continue the rest onto adjacent pages.

If you publish or distribute Opaque copies of the Document numbering more than 100, you must either include a machine-readable Transparent copy along with each Opaque copy, or state in or with each Opaque copy a computer-network location from which the general network-using public has access to download using public-standard network protocols a complete Transparent copy of the Document, free of added material. If you use the latter option, you must take reasonably prudent steps, when you begin distribution of Opaque copies in quantity, to ensure that this Transparent copy will remain thus accessible at the stated location until at least one year after the last time you distribute an Opaque copy (directly or through your agents or retailers) of that edition to the public.

It is requested, but not required, that you contact the authors of the Document well before redistributing any large number of copies, to give them a chance to provide you with an updated version of the Document.

4. MODIFICATIONS

You may copy and distribute a Modified Version of the Document under the conditions of sections 2 and 3 above, provided that you release the Modified Version under precisely this License, with the Modified Version filling the role of the Document, thus licensing distribution and modification of the Modified Version to whoever possesses a copy of it. In addition, you must do these things in the Modified Version:

A. Use in the Title Page (and on the covers, if any) a title distinct from that of the Document, and from those of previous versions (which should, if there were any, be listed in the History section of the Document). You may use the same title as a previous version if the original publisher of that version gives permission.

B. List on the Title Page, as authors, one or more persons or entities responsible for authorship of the modifications in the Modified Version, together with at least five of the principal authors of the Document (all of its principal authors, if it has fewer than five), unless they release you from this requirement.

C. State on the Title page the name of the publisher of the Modified Version, as the publisher.

D. Preserve all the copyright notices of the Document.

E. Add an appropriate copyright notice for your modifications adjacent to the other copyright notices.

F. Include, immediately after the copyright notices, a license notice giving the public permission to use the Modified Version under the terms of this License, in the form shown in the Addendum below.

G. Preserve in that license notice the full lists of Invariant Sections and required Cover Texts given in the Document's license notice.

H. Include an unaltered copy of this License.

I. Preserve the section Entitled "History", Preserve its Title, and add to it an item stating at least the title, year, new authors, and publisher of the Modified Version as given on the Title Page. If there is no section Entitled "History" in the Document, create one stating the title, year, authors, and publisher of the Document as given on its Title Page, then add an item describing the Modified Version as stated in the previous sentence.

J. Preserve the network location, if any, given in the Document for public access to a Transparent copy of the Document, and likewise the network locations given in the Document for previous versions it was based on. These may be placed in the "History" section. You may omit a network location for a work that was published at least four years before the Document itself, or if the original publisher of the version it refers to gives permission.

K. For any section Entitled "Acknowledgements" or "Dedications", Preserve the Title of the section, and preserve in the section all the substance and tone of each of the contributor acknowledgements and/or dedications given therein.

L. Preserve all the Invariant Sections of the Document, unaltered in their text and in their titles. Section numbers or the equivalent are not considered part of the section titles.

M. Delete any section Entitled "Endorsements". Such a section may not be included in the Modified Version.

N. Do not retitle any existing section to be Entitled "Endorsements" or to conflict in title with any Invariant Section.

O. Preserve any Warranty Disclaimers.

If the Modified Version includes new front-matter sections or appendices that qualify as Secondary Sections and contain no material copied from the Document, you may at your option designate some or all of these sections as invariant. To do this, add their titles to the list of Invariant Sections in the Modified Version's license notice. These titles must be distinct from any other section titles.

You may add a section Entitled "Endorsements", provided it contains nothing but endorsements of your Modified Version by various parties—for example, statements of peer review or that the text has been approved by an organization as the authoritative definition of a standard.

You may add a passage of up to five words as a Front-Cover Text, and a passage of up to 25 words as a Back-Cover Text, to the end of the list of Cover Texts in the Modified Version. Only one passage of Front-Cover Text and one of Back-Cover Text may be added by (or through arrangements made by) any one entity. If the Document already includes a cover text for the same cover, previously added by you or by arrangement made by the same entity you are acting on behalf of, you may not add another; but you may replace the old one, on explicit permission from the previous publisher that added the old one.

The author(s) and publisher(s) of the Document do not by this License give permission to use their names for publicity for or to assert or imply endorsement of any Modified Version.

5. COMBINING DOCUMENTS

You may combine the Document with other documents released under this License, under the terms defined in section 4 above for modified versions, provided that you include in the combination all of the Invariant Sections of all of the original documents, unmodified, and list them all as Invariant Sections of your combined work in its license notice, and that you preserve all their Warranty Disclaimers.

The combined work need only contain one copy of this License, and multiple identical Invariant Sections may be replaced with a single copy. If there are multiple Invariant Sections with the same name but different contents, make the title of each such section unique by adding at the end of it, in parentheses, the name of the original author or publisher of that section if known, or else a unique number. Make the same adjustment to the section titles in the list of Invariant Sections in the license notice of the combined work.

In the combination, you must combine any sections Entitled "History" in the various original documents, forming one section Entitled "History"; likewise combine any sections Entitled "Acknowledgements", and any sections Entitled "Dedications". You must delete all sections Entitled "Endorsements."

6. COLLECTIONS OF DOCUMENTS

You may make a collection consisting of the Document and other documents released under this License, and replace the individual copies of this License in the various documents with a single copy that is included in the collection, provided that you follow the rules of this License for verbatim copying of each of the documents in all other respects.

You may extract a single document from such a collection, and distribute it individually under this License, provided you insert a copy of this License into the extracted document, and follow this License in all other respects regarding verbatim copying of that document.

7. AGGREGATION WITH INDEPENDENT WORKS

A compilation of the Document or its derivatives with other separate and independent documents or works, in or on a volume of a storage or distribution medium, is called an "aggregate" if the copyright resulting from the compilation is not used to limit the legal rights of the compilation's users beyond what the individual works permit. When the Document is included in an aggregate, this License does not apply to the other works in the aggregate which are not themselves derivative works of the Document.

If the Cover Text requirement of section 3 is applicable to these copies of the Document, then if the Document is less than one half of the entire aggregate, the Document's Cover Texts may be placed on covers that bracket the Document within the aggregate, or the electronic equivalent of covers if the Document is in electronic form. Otherwise they must appear on printed covers that bracket the whole aggregate.

8. TRANSLATION

Translation is considered a kind of modification, so you may distribute translations of the Document under the terms of section 4. Replacing Invariant Sections with translations requires special permission from their copyright holders, but you may include translations of some or all Invariant Sections in addition to the original versions of these Invariant Sections. You may include a translation of this License, and all the license notices in the Document, and any Warranty Disclaimers, provided that you also include the original English version of this License and the original versions of those notices and disclaimers. In case of a disagreement between the translation and the original version of this License or a notice or disclaimer, the original version will prevail.

If a section in the Document is Entitled "Acknowledgements", "Dedications", or "History", the requirement (section 4) to Preserve its Title (section 1) will typically require changing the actual title.

9. TERMINATION

You may not copy, modify, sublicense, or distribute the Document except as expressly provided for under this License. Any other attempt to copy, modify, sublicense or distribute the Document is void, and will automatically terminate your rights under this License. However, parties who have received copies, or rights, from you under this License will not have their licenses terminated so long as such parties remain in full compliance.

10. FUTURE REVISIONS OF THIS LICENSE

The Free Software Foundation may publish new, revised versions of the GNU Free Documentation License from time to time. Such new versions will be similar in spirit to the present version, but may differ in detail to address new problems or concerns. See http://www.gnu.org/copyleft/.

Each version of the License is given a distinguishing version number. If the Document specifies that a particular numbered version of this License "or any later version" applies to it, you have the option of following the terms and conditions either of that specified version or of any later version that has been published (not as a draft) by the Free Software Foundation. If the Document does not specify a version number of this License, you may choose any version ever published (not as a draft) by the Free Software Foundation.

ADDENDUM: How to use this License for your documents

To use this License in a document you have written, include a copy of the License in the document and put the following copyright and license notices just after the title page:

```
Copyright (C) year your name.
Permission is granted to copy, distribute and/or modify
this document under the terms of the GNU Free
Documentation License, Version 1.2 or any later version
published by the Free Software Foundation; with no
Invariant Sections, no Front-Cover Texts, and no
Back-Cover Texts.  A copy of the license is included in
the section entitled ''GNU Free Documentation License''.
```

If you have Invariant Sections, Front-Cover Texts and Back-Cover Texts, replace the "with...Texts." line with this:

```
with the Invariant Sections being list their
titles, with the Front-Cover Texts being list, and
with the Back-Cover Texts being list.
```

If you have Invariant Sections without Cover Texts, or some other combination of the three, merge those two alternatives to suit the situation.

If your document contains nontrivial examples of program code, we recommend releasing these examples in parallel under your choice of free software license, such as the GNU General Public License, to permit their use in free software.

Index

#

$

-

D

M

N

O

Lightning Source UK Ltd.
Milton Keynes UK
05 August 2010

157936UK00003B/90/A